Today in southern Africa we need many lamps to be lighted to prevent the night from once more reclaiming our land. These lights must take many forms. They must take the forms of actions done, they must take the forms of structures built, they must take the forms of books written, to bring in a new light upon our land. This book, The African Way, marries the soul of Africa to modern business. It is more than helpful. In my many years of travelling all over the earth I have seen that the most powerful nations in the world are those which have married their ancient warrior ethics, philosophy and law to modern business and technology. Like the Japanese, who have brought the Samurai laws to bear on business strategy and labour relations. For this reason I welcome this inspiring book.

– CREDO MUTWA
AFRICAN SPIRITUAL LEADER, AUTHOR, DIVINER, ORAL HISTORIAN

In the evolution of a country, there are but a handful of non-public individuals who positively impact on the process. Mike Boon's journey has put another root into the African earth. With his spiritual and physical commitment, may an enormous number of trees grow to shade future generations.

– DOUG SMOLLAN
INTERNATIONAL PRESIDENT (1994/1995): YOUNG PRESIDENTS' ORGANIZATION
DIRECTOR: SMOLLAN GROUP

There is a marvellous description about today's South Africa early on in Mike Boon's book, The African Way. He writes: 'We are both African and Western and sometimes bits of both. More importantly we have life philosophies, uniquely our own on which our views of the world are founded.' Those words really sum up how a winning company here should go about business. It will search for and arrive at the best combination of management principles to mix with the cultural beliefs and backgrounds of its employees.

– CLEM SUNTER
ANGLO AMERICAN CORPORATION OF SOUTH AFRICA LIMITED

I believe that Mike Boon has joined a small group of people who are making an important contribution to the development of a business and managerial approach that is authentic and relevant to South Africa and its future.

Through his own personal journey and through research and thinking it is clear that many of the ideas that are put forward in The African Way are original and have the potential to make a significant impact to both the debate and the practice of management in South Africa.

– DR NICK BINEDELL
DIRECTOR: WITS BUSINESS SCHOOL

The African Way

The African Way

*The power of
interactive leadership*

Mike Boon

ZEBRA

ZEBRA

Published by Zebra Press
a division of Struik Book Distributors (Pty) Ltd
(a member of the Struik Publishing Group (Pty) Ltd)
32 Thora Crescent, Wynberg, Sandton

Reg.No.: 63/06481/07

First published in August 1996

Editor Hilda Hermann
DTP Marlene Willoughby-Smith
Cover design Neels Bezuidenhout

Reproduction by Disc Express cc, Johannesburg
Printed and bound by CTP Book Printers (Pty) Ltd, PO Box 6060, Parow East 7501

ISBN 1 86870 015 1

Acknowledgements

This book is the product of an almost lifelong journey in search of better leadership and the essence of community and self. Many wonderful people – too numerous to list here – have walked some of this road with me and I thank each of them for their wisdom and challenges.

But the culmination of this journey thus far has been the friendship, stimulation and joy that I have experienced in the development of Group Africa of the Amavulandlela. To each one of the amazing people who make up this dynamic and effective African business community, I offer my sincere thanks.

In particular, I would like to thank the following people: Barry Leitch, Buckey Taylor, Kingsley Holgate, Trevor Penhallrick and John Argyle for all the years that we have spent together and for the learning we have shared.

Johnny Clegg for his assistance on the 'warrior'; Teresa Guzman for her understanding, assistance, care and the many hours of toil; Mr and Mrs Argyle for their kindness in allowing me access to their beautiful retreat in Sedgefield for the writing of this book.

Above all I would like to thank Christine for her unrelenting friendship; for her wisdom, guidance, patience and care.

Contents

INTRODUCTION 11

Part 1

1 FROM WHENCE WE COME 15
African and Western concepts of time 17
The ancestor or the 'shade' 19
Sangomas and nyangas 21

2 A BRIEF HISTORY 25

3 PHILOSOPHY OF THE ABANTU PEOPLE 31
Ubuntu 31
Manifestations of *ubuntu* 33

4 THEN SPEAK TO US OF SELF 35
Seriti/isithunzi 35
The warrior ethic 37
Tribal leadership 44

5 CONFLICT AND CONFUSION IN TRIBE,
FIRST WORLD AND THIRD WORLD 47

Part 2

6 WHAT WE ARE 57
Industrial relations 58
African and Western work groups 59
Tribe, ethnicity and the conflict within 60
Use and misuse of intellect,
communication and behaviour 63

7 THE LAW AND JUSTICE 67
Autocracy, strong leadership and participation 68
Strong leaders 69
Participation 70
The importance of the team 71
Democracy, mob rule and consensus 74

Part 3

8   WHAT WE CAN BECOME 79
    Interactive leadership 80
    Values and principles 84
    Value creation 85

9   THE PATH TO DEMOCRACY AND SHARING 88
    Interactive forums: the *umhlangano* 89
    Democratic value creation 91
    Narrowing the grey 93

10 ACCOUNTABILITY TO SELF 97
    The progression of leadership 98
    Leadership 102

11 ACCOUNTABILITY TO EACH OTHER 106
    Routine *umhlangano* management 108
    Mutual appraisal 112

Part 4

12 DEALING WITH PROBLEMS 117
    Problem 1: Representation 117
    Problem 2: Creeping autocracy 120

Part 5

13 INTERACTIVE LEADERSHIP UNRAVELLED 127

REFERENCES 133
ABOUT THE AUTHOR 135
ABOUT GROUP AFRICA 136
INDEX 138

Introduction

This is a book about revolution in leadership – about people and leadership in a fascinating, complex and challenging workplace: Africa. South Africa has been forged in conflict but also in human triumph. It is a place of multiple cultures – each with their own dramatic and proud histories and powerful heritages. But culture is not static nor is it an isolated thing. It is dynamic and constantly influenced by other groups' thoughts, philosophies and behaviours. So too is leadership.

There is a richness that springs from cross-cultural pollination; attitudes, philosophies and behaviours echo individual cultures, but collectively they are what I call 'Now Africans'.

This book is about leadership in a fascinating and complex environment which covers most of Africa. It is about black Africans and white Africans, white Westerners and black Westerners; it is about the essence of African-ness which is no longer exclusively a thing of blackness but one of humanity and holism. It is about how individual philosophies can be harnessed to create personal fulfilment and business success.

The leadership approaches described in this book have been practised since the early 1980s by a company called Group Africa of the Amavulandlela. The company's phenomenal success bears witness to its powerful and alternate leadership as 'Now African' people.

This book is about Now African people but it is also about the leadership style that is required to lead them. I call this style 'African Interactive Leadership'.

The African Way is divided into five sections. The first two parts lay the foundation and describe the philosophies, belief systems, attitudes and behaviours of 'Now African' people. It tells us who the people are, traditionally and culturally. Much has been written about the West, but black cultures obviously predominate in Africa and need to be understood, for they play a critical role.

Parts three and four look at people in a broader societal context in business itself, and directly explores 'African Interactive Leadership'. Part five draws all of this together.

Note: Although I routinely make use of masculine pronouns for ease of reading, this in no way implies a sexist attitude.

Mike Boon
June 1996

PART 1

CHAPTER 1

▲▲▲▲

From whence we come

Africa is a place of many peoples, many tribes and many beliefs. It is a place of terrible horror and great compassion; one of foolishness and great wisdom. But there is a vision of Africa, based on the nobility and tragedy of the past. This is a land of strong cultures that survive and grow together with the ever-increasing education of proud people, secure in the knowledge that they are the future mentors of the world. The world is beginning to realize that happiness is a state of being and not something we work towards or buy. It is a vision of harmony, prosperity and success; of productive, powerful work teams; of true democracy; of co-operation and interdependence; and of trust and pride in humanity and in each other.

Is it relevant to pursue our African-ness in our global village? The answer to this is simple – Yes! It is supremely relevant in so many ways. We are different people with different cultures. We have our own ways, our own languages, customs, philosophies and beliefs. We have our own history and our own heroes. More importantly, we have our African humanity and our noble cultures. Woe to the world if we all pursue a singular, grey and boring sameness. Our differences and traditions make us interesting and proud.

Every good leader knows of the importance of culture. One talks of 'a culture of violence' or 'a culture of peace'. We create cultures conducive to the achievement of vision, and we all know a culture must precede action. For example, a rigid, slow-moving bureaucracy will not be able to make quick decisions. The bureaucratic culture disallows this. Similarly, a police force with a culture congruent to a military machine, where 'shoot first, ask questions later' is the rule, does not easily use minimal force.

Culture is not an independent thing. It is what we are as people. Our culture guides us in how to behave and it is the expression of our values and beliefs.

If one creates a culture of productivity, efficiency and effectiveness, the economy will thrive automatically. Japan, Malaysia and Singapore are all good examples of this. To create a culture, one does not start with the end point. We should not chase productivity itself. Rather, we should create a culture in which behavioural and attitudinal shifts will result in productivity.

Conscious decisions need to be taken to promote such cultural values and characteristics. For example, the culture of Japan can be described as one of discipline, efficiency and effectiveness. None of this is imposed. It is now a feature – an accepted group of values – every Japanese citizen pursues. One could easily think Japan is an economic power born of historic cultural characteristics. In fact, it is a culture that was purposefully directed. The essence of Japanese success rests on trust, respect and co-operation.

This co-operative spirit is not, as is frequently quoted, a natural or cultural thing. It is the result of years of hard work.
– Productivity SA (MARCH/APRIL 1994)

Culture is, therefore, more important than any other issue. It is the all-embracing force around which everything else revolves.

Have we really given our culture, be it in our business or in our nation, the attention it deserves? At this point in time, our culture is a great melting pot of influences; culture is about borrowing and manifestation. South Africa is in the enviable position of being able to choose which elements to promote as a national and a business culture.

The simplicity of Africa places us in good company.

In spite of the fact that millions of words have been published on Japanese management systems, it comes as a shock to observe first hand not how complicated it all is, but how simple.
– Productivity SA (MARCH/APRIL 1994)

The Americans created a new culture after their own terrible and tragic civil war, the Malaysians did the same after independence, and the Japanese after World War II. In each case, culture was purposefully directed. Africa – particularly South Africa – is poised to, and is in the process of developing an amazing new African culture. Based on traditional tribal African and Western ways, a new African culture has the capability of thrusting us to the forefront of world leadership. In many ways, it already has. Nelson Mandela, son of a rural royal traditionalist, educated both tribally and in the Western way, and honoured by the world for his wisdom and humanity, is a wonderful reflection of that vision for all Africans.

Before we are able to pursue what we can become, we must first know what we are. We are African and Western, ancient and newly born. We are wise and confused, custodians and destroyers. We have black Westerners and white Africans. Our paradigms are African and Western, and sometimes bits of both. More importantly, we have unique life philosophies on which our views of the world are founded. This unique culture, formed out of all of these influences, we will call the 'Now African'.

These uniquely 'Now African' philosophies represent the firm base from which we can move towards the future. Let us explore what we are as Africans in our homes and our cities, in our businesses and our nation.

African and Western concepts of time

Time is valuable and there just isn't enough of it. Time is passing rapidly. Even as you read this, about seven seconds have disappeared and you are probably wondering whether you should quickly scan this page and then look for a few models or concepts that are quick to grasp, and which will help immediately and practically in your life or business. Look no further.

The Western view of time is diametrically opposed to the African view. The difference in the two views of this concept alone illustrates completely different approaches and attitudes to life, humanity, and to work and business. It affects the way we interact with one another, and the difficulty Africans and Westerners sometimes have in understanding the other's motivation and behaviour.

The general Western experience and view of time is based on a lineal concept of time. Time is infinite. For our purposes, let's simply say it started 'in the year dot' and it progresses through the present, into a distant and potentially infinite future. The Western and somewhat futuristic view of time is reflected through expressions such as 'Let bygones be bygones' and 'Tomorrow is another day'. In other words, the past is gone, let's look to the future. This pervades every aspect of the Western psyche. Planning and forecasting for the future consumes us in all aspects of business and in our individual lives. The past is 'history' and is often thought of as boring and something we have to study. It is not a living thing. It is gone. Westerners accept there is an internal locus of control and that, to a considerable degree, one can determine one's future.

The traditional African view is diametrically opposed to this. The African takes a circular view of time, in which the past is more important than the future. The African circles into the past, then the future, and back through the present to the past. There is an acceptance of an external locus of control. In other words, there are forces operating in every person's life over which he or she has absolutely no control. Traditionally, the ancestors play an ongoing and complementary role in every aspect of life.

During 1995, a survey was conducted by Group Africa in rural and urban areas of South Africa. Of 1 637 respondents, 66 per cent said that they believed in the ancestors.

This is interpreted in behavioural issues and is directly related to the African view of time. For example, if something goes wrong in my life now and I am unable to discern anything wrong with my behaviour that could have caused my difficulties, then an unresolved problem must exist somewhere in my ancestry, and it continues to exist in my life. By asking my ancestors to intercede on my behalf, they who are timeless will be able to sort out the problem in the past. As soon as this is done, the current problem will be resolved and the future will take care of itself. No amount of future planning will help.

The black African languages also give us clues to this philosophy. The external locus of control is easily demonstrated through these phrases:

Zulu:	*Ngishiywa itaxi.*	The taxi left me.
Xhosa:	*Ndafelwa yibasi.*	The bus died on me.
English:		I missed the taxi/bus.

A fascinating issue underpinning this attitude to time is the African tradition of *izibongos* (Zulu), *kidiboko* (Sotho) or *isiduko* (Xhosa). These are praise poems, passed through the generations, reciting the great deeds of famous ancestors or great events that affected those ancestors. In this way, the living are informed of the past, and the characteristics of the forefathers, who play such an important and ongoing role in the lives of Africans, are known to all. Excerpts from the *izibongos* of two famous tribal kings are presented below as examples of praise poetry.

Shaka

UShaka! Ngiyesaba ukuti nguShaka.
Ilembe el'eqa amanye amalembe.

UNodum'ehlezi kaMenzi;
uSishaya-kasishayeki.

Inkomo ekala emTonjaneni;
izizwe zonke ziyizwile ukulila.

Translation

Shaka, I fear to even say the name.
The agile one who supersedes the agility of others.
He who thunders even when seated, the striker of blows who is himself unstrikeable.
The bull that bellowed at Mthonjaneni;
All the nations have heard its call.

Moshoeshoe

Nketu ha le sieo mareng a batho,
Beng ba mara ba ntse ba lla, ba re:
Nketu le Ramakoane, le kae.
Ngoan'a Mamokhachane, Thesele
Khomo li kena ka eona, li sa ile.

Thesele, pharu e telele-telele.
Moshaoshoaile, khoaban'a Maphule

Translation

Your praises are poor
when you leave out the warrior.
When you leave out Thesele,
the son of Mokhachane
For it is he who is the warrior of the wars.
Thesele is brave and strong.
That is Moshoeshoe-Moshaila

The impact on business of these fundamentally differing views of time is phenomenal. Needless to say, if Africans and Westerners are to find each other in business and in the country as a whole, they will have to reach out to each other. The African will need to try and grasp the critical importance of the future, punctuality and planning to business. The Westerner will need to try and accept the critical importance of the past (history) to the African.

There are, of course, perversions of other aspects of life that affect time and punctuality. This has to do with discipline, or rather the lack of it, and has nothing whatsoever to do with traditional views of time. The world-renowned author, oral historian and African spiritual leader, Credo Mutwa, had this to say in an interview with the author:

In our African culture there is no such thing as 'African time'. But the people of today escape into laziness and blame our culture. Business was there in Africa, and it was governed by some of the ethics and laws that also govern modern business. For example, let's take a blacksmith. Let's say he promised the king he would deliver certain weapons in 12 days, all complete, sharp and ready. If the order was delivered late, the blacksmith would be fined two cows. Time and discipline were important. If the king said you had to be ready at the first moment of milking, you could not arrive at midday. Africans respected time, and honesty in traditional business was the norm.

Bearing in mind the African view of time and the importance of the ancestors, the next section will briefly look at who and what the ancestors are, how we communicate with them, our people's stories or history, and the famous leaders from the early days of modern South Africa.

The ancestor or the 'shade'

Should we use the word 'ancestor' here, the impression may be that these are people who have lived before and who are now dead. More importantly, it would imply a separateness between the living and the dead. To avoid this, we will use the term 'shade' as this assumes an intimacy with the living – an ongoing relationship that does not cease with death.

All the tribal peoples of southern Africa, and those of Bantu origin in Central, West and East Africa, come from a tradition in which the shades have been fundamental to life. In the past, it was primarily the missionaries who sought to eradicate this life view, believing erroneously that the ancestors competed with God. It was believed by the church that ancestor worship was evil and it was attacked mercilessly. Of course, this had a further effect. Sangomas (diviners) are spirit-mediums through whom the living can communicate with the shades. Sangomas were viewed as evil priests and priestesses by the church and they became known as witchdoctors. This drove them into the twilight world of in-between people who were needed but could not be recognized by a society that feared the wrath of the church.

There are varying degrees of belief in who the shades are and their roles and powers. There is general acceptance and accommodation of traditional and religious concepts. Many people who are Christians, and who attend church regularly, also accept the presence of the shades. Examples of this synergy can be seen in the African Zionist Church and the Shembe sects, but this also applies to people who are Methodist, Anglican or Muslim. There is no conflict in this. The shades, they say, are like saints are to Christians – good people who have gone before. The difference, of course, is that Africans know the shades are always with us and can be spoken to, whereas saints are people who have lived but are no longer with us. Even here, though, there is conflict because Christians readily accept that a person can be possessed by an evil spirit – to the point where, in extreme cases, the church will perform an exorcism. Surely this acknowledges the presence of spirits? In the African way, all people, good and bad, become spirits. These spirits are called different things and are treated differently. The good spirits become shades, whereas the bad ones remain 'lost'. Perhaps angels are the closest things to which Westerners can relate in their own life view.

It is not everyone who qualifies to become an idlozi *(a shade). If I was a very bad person, and I stole goats and was cruel to my wife, or if I was ill-treating the cattle and the children, then I don't qualify to be* idlozi. *Rather, I will be called* isamfumfu – *a lost, evil spirit. That spirit will not be honoured. Although the* isamfumfu *is evil, we must never allow it to fade away from us because then it may curse us. So we must do ceremonies for the* isamfumfu. *But we must not say why we are killing the goat or for whom we are making this beer. And when we place the beer for the* isamfumfu, *we must walk out backwards.'*

– CREDO MUTWA

So it is only the good who qualify to become shades. As people would never presume to talk directly to God, the shades become the messengers between the living and God.

The place of the shades is in the cattle enclosure, where one may call on them. When doing so, blood is let from a sheep or a goat, depending on the culture group. In urban areas, chickens are slaughtered. Only in extreme cases of difficulty or death will an ox or a bull be slaughtered.

I have attended many ceremonies that, except for blood-letting, have been conducted entirely inside the great or ancestral hut *(indlu kamadlozi)*. The shades are believed to be near the back of the hut, at the *umsamu*. In urban areas, this is replaced in interesting ways.

Not having access to a traditionally structured home is not regarded as problematic. I attended a ceremony in an urban township to *jabulisa* (encourage/make happy) the shades for an aged friend and mentor, during which a slaughter took place. The goat was presented in the lounge and then slaughtered outside. The meat was then wrapped in the skin and kept overnight in the man's bedroom. The shades were addressed in the lounge with the *umbeko* (choice parts of the slaughtered animal), as is tradition, being used to appease the shades.

There are several ways in which the shades reveal themselves and their wishes to people. One of the most common ways is through dreams. These can be extremely powerful revelations which may seriously disturb some people.

The importance of the shades to ordinary people is evident in the expressions we hear being used when things go wrong. There is for example, the Sotho saying *Badimo bahau baho furuletse* (The ancestors/shades have turned their backs on me). This implies they no longer have a say in their lives. This type of expression is also present in other languages.

Certain cultures are respected and acknowledged in business, and considerable efforts are made to accommodate Christian, Hindu, Jewish and other religious festivals and idiosyncrasies. For example, in a company with a predominantly Jewish or Muslim workforce, it is unlikely that pork would appear on the canteen menu.

The great irony is that we are in Africa. The majority of the workforce is African, but there is enormous ignorance of African customs and beliefs – even of something as significant as belief in the shades.

Nonetheless, the shades play a crucial and ongoing role in many people's lives in both rural and urban areas. Because of the negative stigma that has been attached to this belief in the past, caused primarily by arrogant colonial and religious intolerance, many people deny any knowledge of or belief in the shades. It is the very people who were once shunned by society, the sangomas, who are able to tell of the people – from collar-and-tie businessmen to peasant labourers – who creep in to visit them after dark, so none of their friends will see. In many respects, this is not too dissimilar to the rather private attitude Westerners maintain when visiting a psychologist.

Sangomas and nyangas

In later chapters we will explore the differences in the African and the Western philosophical approaches to life in some depth. But at this stage, it is important to point out that Westerners tend to view 'self' in very clear, existential categories: body, soul, mind and spirit. Each part which helps to make up the whole has its own healing needs. When unwell, Westerners call in specialists: a physician, a minister of religion, rabbi or priest, a psychologist or psychiatrist, and many others. The traditional African approach is far more holistic and the parts less pronounced. Healing is approached holistically and is the role of the sangoma. In societies in which the shades are a feature of life, health is a function of such holism. A sangoma is a diviner and a herbalist – a type of priest-healer.

But the myth of the witchdoctor persists. Sangomas and nyangas are not witchdoctors. Sangomas do not choose this profession for themselves. They experience a calling from the shades who come to them in their dreams. They are powerless to resist this call, for if they do they will be punished by the shades for their disrespect, become ill and may even die. For the cynics, let me assure you this does happen. I have personally witnessed such things. In the dreams, the shades guide those who have been called to the home of a sangoma who will become their mentor. During training, the individual or initiate is known as a *thwasa,* and is shown all the uses of medicinal plants and herbs by the shades in dreams.

The teacher or mentor to whom the *thwasa* is apprenticed, will train the *thwasa* in the various rituals and dances that form an integral part of being a sangoma. For example, the *intlombe* or *xhentsa* rituals of the Xhosa form the core of the healing process among the people of the area, and the mentor trains the *thwasa* in these. But the shades reveal the wisdom of herbal medicines to the *thwasa* themselves. This is the primary difference between a sangoma and a *nyanga.* A nyanga is a herbalist or, if you prefer, a naturopath. The *thwasa* has no divination capabilities and is apprenticed to a nyanga to learn the skills of the profession.

Here is an actual example of how an ordinary person can be affected:

Mary is a successful representative for Group Africa and has worked for the company for about six years. She is a well-educated, confident person who was born and raised in an urban area. One day she had an accident while driving her vehicle. Having never had an accident before, she was understandably shaken. Fortunately, no one was hurt and her vehicle was only slightly damaged. She was soon back to her old confident self, making calls and visiting clients.

Shortly after the accident, Mary had a second one. This time she sustained light injuries and was off work for a week or so to recover. Her colleagues of every culture group, black and white, rallied around to support and help her in every way they could. Her confidence was quite badly shaken, but she decided she was fit and well enough to resume work.

Then she had a third, far more serious accident. She ended up in hospital with a fractured sternum, broken ribs, lacerations, and a host of other problems. It was at this time she started to talk to me about the shades and searched in her mind for what she had done to anger them. She had never mentioned the shades or talked of sangomas previously, but now, under the ever-worsening circumstances in her life, she was beginning to say: *'Idlozi lifulatele'* (The ancestors have turned their backs on me). When she was eventually released from hospital and returned to work, it was only to say she could no longer work or drive a vehicle.

Rather than allow her to leave the group, I held discussions with her to search for solutions. One of the solutions was for her to visit a sangoma. Mary disappeared to Mpumalanga for nearly ten days with her company vehicle and a driver we supplied because of her fear of driving.

When she returned, she was her old confident, happy and secure self. She was driving willingly and unhesitatingly, and a small bag of *muti* (medicine/herbs) hung under the vehicle's steering column. She was even walking more upright, strongly and with purpose. The sangoma had healed her and the shades were appeased. Her body was healing fast and her spirit was at peace.

Mary has not had another accident and, although she no longer has the *muti* in her vehicle, she is at peace with herself because the shades are at peace.

The point of this story is simple. Even people one would never expect to act in a particular way or believe certain things, may well do so, especially in times of stress. There is no denying the existence of such belief systems, or of the sangomas who can cure or heal when the need arises. They do exist, they play a very important role in people's lives, and they need to be accommodated in our businesses. Indeed, you probably have a sangoma or a nyanga working in your business right now! In a recent national survey by Group Africa, comprising 1 100 people in both urban and rural areas of South Africa, 50 per cent of the respondents said sangomas played an important role in their lives. This obviously implies acceptance of and belief in the existence of the shades.

A full-time sangoma can be visited in his *ndomba* (traditional rooms), but there are many other sangomas who lead normal, everyday lives, and who practise in the evenings or during weekends. Here are some examples:

Frank has been a successful manager in a company for about nine years. He dresses in Western fashion collar-and-tie for work and has a very busy schedule, staff to look after, and appointments to keep.

But Frank has another life. He is a sangoma called by a particular shade – his great grandfather – who was also a sangoma. Occasionally, he experiences difficulties with this apparently dual existence. For example, recently he had a seizure, fell down in the office, frothing at the mouth, his body jerking and twisting uncontrollably. When he came round he looked dazed and far away, but he knows it is not epilepsy or any other discernible illness. In fact, it's not an illness at all – it is the shades calling him. In this instance, Frank was being punished by the ancestors. He had not let them know he had moved to a new house and he had not done a traditional welcome for the shades. In addition, although he is not permitted to eat pork, he had done so. And, he had allowed some friends to sleep in the *ndomba*, where he conducts various ceremonies with the shades and keeps his medicines.

All of these things had displeased the shades. None of this is spoken about openly, and most people think he suffers from fits. If the seizures at work become too severe, Frank knows he will have to leave and practise divining full time. At the moment, he is able to accommodate all of these factors in his life.

Gloria is in public relations for the travel industry – welcoming guests, seeing to their needs, and gently bullying them when necessary. She is a strong, sensitive and kind woman, whom people like immediately. Her warmth is tangible. She initially trained as a nursing sister, worked for many years in a large hospital, and qualified in maternity, surgery and intensive care.

When she was about 40 years old, she was called to be a sangoma. She left her nursing career and became a *thwasa*. Once qualified, she practised full time, but eventually decided to follow two careers. Recognizing that nursing would not allow for the flexibility she required, she took a job in an environment where her hours would be more routine, and in which she would be able to keep the shades happy by also practising as a sangoma.

The sangomas are the links or the mediums that ordinary people can use to interact with the shades. The past is not distant or separate, as the shades are the past and they dwell together with us in the present.

CHAPTER 2

▲▲▲▲

A brief history

The 30-year period between 1810 and 1840 was a time of unbelievable conflict and turmoil in southern Africa. This was a time that saw the emergence, consolidation or clear establishment of practically every 'modern' tribal group in the subcontinent. This entire period is known as the Mfecane in the coastal region and Difaqane in the interior. The pressures caused by excruciating hardships and bloody wars created a fertile zone for the emergence of great leaders, the fathers and mothers of our nation – the leaders and people from which much of our national culture is derived.

Ancestry is crucial in the understanding of tribal groupings, but it is not a subject that can be covered lightly or glibly. What follows is a meagre summary for the busy reader of some of the most important events to have left their marks on the subcontinent. You are encouraged to explore these in much greater detail.

In the region of the Great Fish River in the Eastern Cape, first Boer and then British settlers clashed with Xhosa-speaking people. Famous leaders, such as Ngqika, Sandile and Maqoma, emerged as powerful leaders. Indeed, Maqoma, one of the most revered Tembu leaders, was part of a sad process affecting many great national leaders that only terminated in the early 1990s: arrest and incarceration on Robben Island.

Around 1806, in what is now known as KwaZulu-Natal, a man called Dingiswayo became paramount chief of the Mthetwa people. It was he who first employed the regimental system which was later to be refined, developed and used to devastating effect by Shaka, the founder and most famous king of the modern Zulu nation.

Immediately north of Dingiswayo, another great leader, Zwide, was consolidating his power base among the Ndwandwe people. And still further north, in what is now known as Swaziland, Sobhuza was doing the same among the amaNgwane (Swazi).

North of this area, a horrific human tragedy had been taking place for some years. Traders, which included Brazilians and Portuguese, were establishing vigorous dealings in ivory, cattle and slaves. Making use of Delagoa Bay (Maputo, Mozambique) as their base, these slave-traders inflicted terrible and inhumane devastation inland of the port.

There was, it has been estimated, a loss to slavers of between 25 and 50 per cent of the entire male population of the Delagoa Bay hinterland.
– Noël Mostert, *Frontiers*

Survivors of this despicable trade fled inland, to an unsettled area. Far in the Northern Cape and what is now known as the Free State, the Griqua and other mixed-blood groups were creating havoc through constant and violent cattle raiding. To escape these raids, the Tswana and Sotho people were forced east and north on to one another's land, and more clashes occurred. The ripple effect of this was felt by tribes right across to the eastern frontiers with the Nguni people.

At Delagoa Bay, British and American whalers were adding to the demands on the area. They, of course, needed meat to feed their sailors. In order to supply those who were hungry for ivory and cattle, Northern Natal, which was rich in both aspects, became a focal point. Many minor chiefs, who were anxious to participate in the lucrative trade that would net them beads, brass and cloth, began to clash, and hunting parties took on the appearance of military expeditions.

In addition, it is possible that Natal felt the effects of overgrazing and too frequent and unseasonal veld fires, which reduced the carrying capacity for cattle and added to the competition for grazing.

Gradually, weaker chiefs became incorporated under larger, more powerful ones, and it was in this environment that Dingiswayo, Zwide and Sobhuza asserted themselves.

After Dingiswayo's death, Shaka gained total control of the Mthethwa and Zulu peoples. During this period, he designed a weapon for his armies that is feared to this day: the *ikhwa* – a broad-bladed, short-shafted spear, similar to the Roman broadsword, that was responsible for the deaths of hundreds of thousands of people.

It was not long before Shaka set his mind to adjusting the tactics of war and its weapons. This change was the famous chest-and-horns formation which he used successfully to vanquish his enemies. It was simple, effective and bloody. The formation would approach the enemy in a box-like group. As it struck the enemy, the warriors to the sides (or the 'horns') would suddenly free themselves and sprint around the enemy, encircling and crushing, completely destroying everything in their grip.

Soon Shaka had decimated his northern neighbours, the Ndwandwe, and his Zulu armies were the undisputed power in a region extending from the Tugela River in the south, to the Pongola in the north, and the Buffalo in the west. His expansionist policies had a further devastating effect on the region. In the south, all the way to the Umtata River, people gradually lost everything to the Zulus – their cattle, their ability to raise crops (which were constantly taken by foraging Zulu armies), their young women and, eventually, their dignity. Henry Francis

Fynn, who travelled through the area at that time, wrote of emaciated and desperate people, who were dirty, terrified and, in some instances, turning to cannibalism as their only means of survival. Thus began a period of migration of people who fled from Shaka and tyranny, as he raided and terrorized the tribes bordering Zululand.

One of the migrating groups was led by Soshangane, who was to found the Shangaan nation. Mzilikazi was another leader, who founded the powerful Ndebele nation, and the effect of yet another leader, Zwangendaba, was felt as far away as what is now recognized as Zambia and Malawi. These groups and others like them – for example, the amaNgwane led by Matiwane, and the amaHlubi led by Mpangazitha – created havoc wherever they moved.

The latter two groups moved over the Drakensberg and clashed with the Batlokwa tribe, led by the famous queen regent, Manthatisi. Their attacks were so furious that Manthatisi and her followers were forced to abandon all their possessions and flee. They, in turn, encountered people inhabiting the streams flowing into the upper Vaal River, and drove them from their land.

So chaotic and rapid was the movement that, within a very short space of time, many of the remnants of smaller tribes had begun to mass under Manthatisi's leadership in search of relative security. These people made up a vast horde and this massive force moved up, down and around the Caledon River, completely disrupting and devastating the Sotho tribes in the area. So great was Manthatisi's reputation and so considerable was the terror she created, that her name was used by victims to describe their assailants. Another enormous group, fleeing from the chaos in the south, led by, among others, three Southern Sotho chiefs – Nkgarahanye, Tshane and Sebetwane – crossed the Vaal River and moved northwest, destroying everything in its path.

The rumour spread of the approach of an invincible army led by a gigantic woman who had a single eye in her forehead, and who fed her followers with her own milk. The tribes in the line of advance were so terrified by these tales that they made no attempt to band together and resist. In the south, Manthatisi maintained the group's strength by forcing captured enemies to become part of her horde. Many people were killed and some 28 distinct tribes were, apparently, completely obliterated.

Refugees began arriving in the Cape Colony and appeared on the northernmost farms as shrunken skeletons covered with skin and in a desperate state. Assembled together and fed by the *landdrosts*, these people were then apprenticed to farmers, many of them British settlers in the Albany area.

Excepting these and the clan of the Bataung under the chief Makwana, who managed to hide away for a time, the whole of the Bantu inhabitants of the territory between the Vaal and the head waters of the Caledon passed out of existence.
– George THEAL, *History of Southern Africa 1795–1872*

While this was happening, the amaHlubi and amaNgwane continued fighting each other and the people living south of the Caledon River. Many people were killed in these bloody clashes. In a short time, all the cattle were eaten and, as nothing had been cultivated, a terrible famine arose. Tens of thousands of people perished from starvation. Thousands fled, and many of those who remained behind were forced to turn to cannibalism. The Bafokeng are believed to be the first group who turned to this practice, but it was by no means confined only to them. Initially, it was the Bushmen who were hunted down in their mountain retreats for food. When no more could be found, the cannibals began on people of their own tribe.

In the coastal area to the east of the Drakensberg things were not much better. Before this terrible period, the areas between the Tugela and Umzimvubu rivers were the most densely populated in South Africa. But one after another the tribes here were attacked, overpowered and ruined.

A great horde of fugitives, mostly Bhaca, gradually made their way south under the leadership of a chief known as Madikane. He was resting and feasting his people near the source of the Umgwali River when, before daylight on 20 December 1824, he was attacked by a combined force of Tembu and Xhosa, led by Vusani and Hintsa. Madikane was killed and his people fled. Suddenly, it became dark and the stars became visible.

The people were terrified, and the Tembu and Xhosa victors began to disperse in disarray, believing the darkness to be caused by the powerful chief Madikane's death. But soon thereafter, the sun began to shine – it had been a solar eclipse.

The Bhaca horde dispersed and its remnants became vassals of the Xhosa and Tembu people. This is how some of the amaBhele, amaZizi, Abasekunene and amaHlubi managed to survive. These people and their descendants now make up the Mfengu (Fingo) people of the Eastern Cape. The word 'Mfengu' is derived from the word *uKufenguza* (to wander about seeking shelter).

Out of this chaotic state, tribal groupings were gradually consolidated and new ones were formed. For example, the formation of the Southern Sotho nation was a direct result of the upheavals.

One needs to stop and reflect on the turmoil and horror of the period to fully appreciate its significance.

Moshoeshoe's own grandfather, Peete, was captured and eaten by cannibals near the town of Leribe, situated in northern Lesotho.

Moshoeshoe took his people southwest to a mountain called Thaba-Bosigo (mountain of the night), a natural fortress which proved to be impregnable for many years. Initially ousting the Baputi clan from the area, Moshoeshoe then concentrated on strengthening this well-watered and critical mountain stronghold. Great boulders were piled on the tops of the few passes and along the cliff-tops, ready to be hurled down on any approaching enemy. He then led his people in several expeditions against the powerful Batlokwa (under Manthatisi and her son, Sikonyela) and the amaHlubi of Mpangazitha. His successes against these formidable enemies gained him considerable fame as a strategist, and many people joined him. He was able to continue attracting people because of his success in keeping his own herds and increasing them through raids. This occurred simultaneously with the total devastation and starvation elsewhere.

Unlike other leaders of the time, Moshoeshoe accepted people who had been hostile to him into his ever-expanding tribe. Most of them arrived destitute, but he allocated them land and loaned them cattle. Even great bands of cannibals were induced to join him and, like others, received cattle on loan. This was known as the *Mafisa* system. Although the cattle belonged to Moshoeshoe, the group concerned could take the milk as their own. In this way, Moshoeshoe's wealth grew as the herds did, but the people under his control were also well fed and cared for. He maintained a loose overlordship that relied on diplomatic and leadership abilities rather than coercion.

Moshoeshoe established ties with Shaka, and by so doing gained a very powerful ally against Matiwane, who was still the regional power. In 1827, Matiwane was driven out of the area by a Zulu army and, after the army's return to Zululand, relative calm prevailed. The fact that Moshoeshoe, in a time of great turmoil and upheaval, was able to weld together considerably diverse groups into a single cohesive and proud nation, is one of the most remarkable achievements of the Difaqane. The Southern Sotho people can be justly proud of their illustrious ancestor.

Another group that formed at this time was the Ndebele under Mzilikazi. They eventually controlled a massive tract of land extending northwards from the Vaal River, where they remained until 1836. Then the tribe known as the Boers or Afrikaners began to approach the Ndebele border. They were in the early stages of what became known as the Great Trek – a migration of Afrikaners away from the Cape and British rule. A significant series of clashes occurred between the two groups.

I will briefly relate the first of these clashes as an illustration of how differently the same event can be viewed depending on cultural perspective.

The Boers arrived and stopped at the Vaal River, whereupon a group under Hendrik Potgieter was sent forward to reconnoitre. A Boer named Stephanus Erasmus, independent of the Voortrekkers, decided to make use of the presence of the Trekkers along the Vaal and organized a hunting trip into Mzilikazi's territory. He hunted in an area designated as the king's own royal hunting ground. The Ndebele reaction was quick and ruthless. Discovering the hunting party and their booty-laden wagons, they attacked, killing all but Erasmus and one son who was hunting with him. Thinking of the Trekkers now scattered along the banks of the Vaal, Erasmus galloped off with his son to warn them. He came across the Botha and Steyn families in the present-day Parys area and blurted out a warning.

As soon as they could, the Voortrekkers gathered and formed a laager at a place now known as Vegkop (Battle Hill) between the Renoster and Wilge rivers, and awaited the attack they knew would follow. In this laager, there were only 40 men or boys capable of using firearms, one of whom was a 12-year-old boy destined for great fame later in his life as president of the Boer Transvaal republic – Paul Kruger.

On the afternoon of 15 October 1836, a great Ndebele army, some 6 000 strong, approached. Both sides waited out the night, and it can only be imagined what thoughts entered the minds of all those brave Africans that night. The leader of the Ndebele force was Mkalipi who, for some reason, did not employ normal Ndebele tactics of night attack. Instead, he waited until the next day when the sun was already high before initiating the assault. After three massive attacks on the wagons, each one seemingly more vigorous and terrible than the last, the Ndebele withdrew. To this day, the battle at Vegkop is celebrated as a massive Voortrekker victory.

But there is also a different view, which comes to us through the *izibongos* of the Ndebele. The story agrees with everything – except the result. After three massive assaults on the wagons, the Ndebele army withdrew to a great Ndebele victory, because they left with 4 600 cattle, 100 horses and 53 000 sheep. After all, what is the purpose of war if not for booty?

This illustrates how cultural interpretations can provide dramatically different views of an event. We need to be constantly aware of this in our business environments.

Subsequent to this famous battle, the Voortrekkers put together a powerful army and invaded Mzilikazi's domain. In this way, another of the great leaders and progenitors during the time of the Mfecane was driven from the Transvaal and replaced by the Boers. Over the next three years, Mzilikazi's followers remained split into two broad groups, each one unaware of the whereabouts of the other. Eventually they came together in the area of what is now Bulawayo in Zimbabwe. Mzilikazi re-established himself here and maintained his reputation as a major ruler of the subcontinent.

Tribes were formed or resettled on new lands. Alliances were formed, attitudes of one group to another were consolidated, and the repercussions of these can be felt to this day in the country and the workplace.

It is important to recognize that this is an extremely controversial period of history and as much study as possible should be made to gain a clear insight into what actually occurred.

Without doubt, the great leaders of this period are honoured and revered as some of the most important ancestors of our nation.

CHAPTER 3

Philosophy of the abantu people

South Africa has been forged in conflict. Good examples of this are the Mfecane and Lifaqane wars. But these represent only a brief period in a series of tragedies and conflicts that have occurred almost continuously for hundreds of years. The most recent and well known is, of course, apartheid itself. Through all of these conflicts there has been a gradual cultural meltdown – a mutation of classic culture and philosophy that has left a variety of cultural expressions in individual tribes. This vast cultural range is even more complex when viewing the entire cross-tribal spectrum of our diverse peoples.

To understand the people that make up this fascinating continent, and who work in our businesses, we need to understand the great range of influences, cultures and philosophies that consciously or otherwise affect every African. Philosophically, there are certain classic platforms on which our existing ethics, beliefs and behaviours are based. Are Africans and Westerners different in this arena, or is this a place where merging has occurred? Is the human philosophical basis important to us in business, leadership and life?

People are life and business, and by not understanding our people, we are destined to remain in conflict. By examining philosophy and culture at play, we can learn why people act and think in a particular way.

Ubuntu

The heritage of the philosophy that comes to us through our traditional African roots is *ubuntu*: morality, humaneness, compassion, care, understanding and empathy. It is one of sharing and hospitality, of honesty and humility. Simply put, it is the ethic and interaction that occurs in the extended family. In Africa, it draws in all of the people. In this 'family' there is a community of shared values and equality.

Ubuntu is best described through the expression: *Umuntu ngumuntu ngabantu* (Zulu), *Umutu ke mutu ke batho* (Sotho), *Umundu nimudu niunde wa andu*

(Kikuyu), *Munhu munhu pamusana pevanhu* (Shona). All of these mean: A person is only a person because of other people. This is the philosophy of *ubuntu* (Zulu) or *batho* (Sotho). Rank means nothing unless one's spirit and humanity are of the same stature.

Ubuntu is not empirical. It does not exist unless there is interaction between people in a community. It manifests through the actions of people, through truly good things that people unthinkingly do for each other and for the community. One's humanity can, therefore, only be defined through interaction with others.

It is believed the group is as important as the individual, and a person's most effective behaviour is in the group. All efforts working towards this common good are lauded and encouraged, as are all acts of kindness, compassion and care, and the great need for human dignity, self-respect and integrity.

As indicated previously, our language is able to reflect our philosophies. Here are several examples of proverbs in which the philosophy of *ubuntu* is very apparent:

Southern Sotho
Ntja pedi hae hlowhe he sebata.

Translation
It is better to do things as a group than as an individual.

Xhosa
Intaka yokha ngentsiba lenye intaka.

Translation
A bird builds its house with another bird's feather.

Zulu
Isisu somhamb'asingakanani.

Translation
The stomach of a traveller is small.

In a strange place, a traveller need only announce himself to a household as a stranger and that he is hungry. The people of the home will always give him what they can and will constantly excuse themselves for being unable to give him more.

Xhosa
Izandla ziyahlambana.

Translation
The hands wash each other.

People are interdependent; without each other we cannot achieve.

Pedi
Go fa ke go fega.

Translation
Giving is to dish out for oneself.

Although the emphasis of this proverb is on the reciprocity of kindness, it is important to emphasize the African view of favours. Should one offer kindness, it is understood the individual may never be able to reciprocate. However, life's way is that one day someone, somewhere, will return this kindness.

Zulu

Umuzi ngumuzi ngokuphanjukelwa.   A home is a real one if people visit it.

This implies a home is welcoming and happy, and that people will wish to visit it because of this. Strangers will always be made to feel welcome.

All of these proverbs, and many more, demonstrate the innate encouragement that all people give to those offering care, kindness, empathy, sharing and humaneness. There is also a clear community of shared values and equality as 'a person is only a person because of other people'.

To a considerable degree, a Westerner's view of life, ethics and values are based on Greco-Roman philosophy entwined with Judaic and Christian religious beliefs. The latter is true even of atheists, who are still haunted by the values, if not the religious beliefs concerned. For example, 'Thou shalt not kill' and 'Thou shalt not steal' are definitive laws and values society adheres to irrespective of religious belief. 'Love thy neighbour', however, becomes a subjective value assessment. How far does this love/care go? What exactly does it mean? But it is generally accepted as a good aspirational ethic, regardless of its religious base.

The order in the universe as recorded by Aristotle and Plato continues to affect the Western approach to life. It is here that one begins to see the most significant diversion from African thought. The Western philosophy of humanism, itself emanating from the Renaissance, is based on the Greco-Roman premise of man as a rational being. It intellectualizes the concept of humanity and, in so doing, makes it individual – something one can choose to follow if one accepts the rationale. African *ubuntu* does none of this. It simply exists. It is moral and good. It is emotional and deep, and people simply act in a way they intuitively know to be right. It is not something one chooses, and it is accepted as the way life is.

Manifestations of *ubuntu*

Forming part of the philosophy of *ubuntu* is openness, sharing and welcome. This is demonstrated in many ways and particularly through weddings. In traditional African society there are open weddings. Everyone in the community is aware of the engagement as it is publicly announced by the raising of a white flag. The wedding date is then carefully monitored. On the day, anyone who would like to, comes to the wedding. But people do not arrive empty-handed. Besides the gifts for the bridal couple, they bring beer and food and they join in the celebration.

In Western society, the exact opposite is true. There is a specific number of guests and a wedding is an exclusive affair. Indeed, in many instances there is a fair amount of arguing as to who should or should not be invited.

Because of the inclusive and empathetic way of life among traditional Africans, orphans and problem children are drawn into society, and absorbed into other families. In this way they are cared for, nurtured, given love and develop as full and active members of the community. Everyone becomes the mother, father, brother or sister of these children.

The Western way is to isolate orphans and problem children in orphanages and homes, where it is believed they will be fully cared for by professionals. Unfortunately, this often means the children are separated from normal, everyday society and are not easily integrated at a later stage. This is directly related to Western society's inability to offer 'personal family' social support, which is a function of the unitary family.

The Western unitary family is one in which the individual is paramount. Individual competition is encouraged. The African environment displays the extended family ethic in which there is a superordinate goal for the collective to aspire to. In other words, unlike the Western model which is focused on the individual, the African tribal model is focused on the group. Because of the collective approach in the African tribal way, each individual has recourse to innumerable support structures. One seldom, if ever, hears of family murders, sexual perversion or incest. The closest one will come to the latter is marriage between cousins (which is culturally acceptable among certain Sotho groups).

The entire family, which is much wider than the Western nuclear family and includes married brothers and cousins, is involved in all relationships. In real terms, marriage is a contract between two families and not two individuals as in the Western way. Because of this, the family remains involved in the individual's relationship. Everything is everyone's business, so it is practically impossible for problems to build up to a critical point where, for example, a family murder occurs, without the extended family being aware of and diffusing the danger. One begins to see these problems in urban and transitional people, where the fabric of society has been eroded and has not been replaced with another community.

A community is made up of individuals who are all independent but interdependent. It is not an amorphous mass. A powerful community is made up of powerful individuals. *Ubuntu* is only possible because of the individuals in the group.

Ubuntu can be harnessed in the nation-building process and in the workplace. The *tirelo sechaba* (to work for the community) system in Botswana is a direct and wonderful example this. Prior to enrolling for their own studies at university, young urban students are encouraged to spend as much as a year in less privileged rural communities, sharing their knowledge with their country cousins.

By gaining a full and deep understanding of the cultural and philosophical basis of the people in a business team or community, one is better able to harness their energies. One can synergize the march to a shared vision and fully comprehend interdependence. Without a deep cultural empathy, this cannot be comfortably, efficiently, effectively or happily realized.

CHAPTER 4

Then speak to us of self

Seriti/isithunzi

A critical base to traditional African philosophy is known as *seriti* (Sotho) or *isithunzi* (Nguni). The origin of the word *seriti,* in its form *moriti,* means shade or shadow, but it is seen as the vital life-force identifying an individual. It is part of all life, but it is also personal, intimately affected by and affecting other forces.

Seriti is thought of as an aura around a person – a physical thing. '*Seriti* is the energy or power that both makes us ourselves and unites us in personal interaction with others.' (Schutte: *Philosophy for Africa*). In the words of Temples, in *Bantu Philosophy, seriti* is 'a vital force, at this very time to be in intimate and personal relationship with other forces acting above him and below him in the hierarchy of forces.'

Although there is considerable emphasis on the individual and self, this needs to be seen in relation to all other life. While *seriti* identifies an individual, it does not exist unless it is seen in the context of its interaction with the community of life-forces.

One's *seriti* or *isithunzi* reflects one's moral weight, influence and prestige. It is what identifies us to be good or, indeed, what will identify us as depleted of goodness. The more good deeds one does in life, the more one shares humanity, and the greater one's *seriti* grows. If we do bad or evil, our *seriti* is reduced. This is demonstrated in the well-known Sotho expression, *O tlosa seriti* (You are taking away your shadow), which is said whenever someone does something bad.

Idlozi (the shade) and isithunzi/seriti *are interchangeable. The* seriti/isithunzi *is sometimes called an aura. We Africans believe the* isithunzi, *which after death becomes an* idlozi, *is shaped by the appearance and the experiences of the person of the physical being. This* isithunzi, *the little soul, is not immortal. If you neglect it, it will slowly fade away.*

– CREDO MUTWA

Seriti is directly associated with clan names and characteristics, and is made up to a significant degree by the good deeds of one's ancestors. It is this weight of generations that is enormously important in life. One often hears comments about a family or clan that has a good *seriti: 'O tlosa motse wa hao seriti'* (You are taking the [good] shadow away from your [good] home.) A good home, of course, has a good shadow.

Seriti can best be visualized as being broken up into lots of little *seritis*. For example, there is one for the clan, one for family lineage and another for self. The clan and lineage *isithunzi's* have the weight of generations behind them and will not be changed dramatically by an individual's personal status in life. But a personal *seriti/isithunzi* remains a reflection of personal goodness and humanity. So even a person without noble ancestry can engender great personal *seriti* during his life. This is passed on to the next generation and the clan and family name is enhanced.

Seriti or *isithunzi* can perhaps explain why Nelson Mandela, after nearly three decades in jail, does not seek revenge and persecution of his jailers. Were he to do this, he would be taking away from the goodness that comes through forgiveness, and in this way his *seriti* would be reduced. By forgiving and seeking conciliation – by doing what is good – his life-force, his *seriti* and, therefore, the *seriti* of his family and clan, even the nation, is enhanced.

There is, however, a sharper, harder side in the development of *seriti/isithunzi*, which often arises through the trauma of war and conflict. Individuals, groups and even nations have been known to overcome apparently impossible obstacles. They do this selflessly and with great courage, which results in the growth and development of their *seriti/isithunzi*. If you have ever met a person who has been recognized, perhaps publicly, for a deed of great courage, possibly in time of war, you will know of the aura that surrounds him.

What is the *seriti/isithunzi* of your team and the individuals who comprise it? What is your own and how has it been formed through your life deeds?

By making the effort to explore the individual, family and clan histories of the people who work with or for you, you are, in effect, offering a great compliment. You show that you are attempting to understand the substance of an individual and gaining a measure, through his ancestry (which is crucial in the African way), of his *isithunzi*.

As in all businesses, Group Africa has to deal with competition. Some years ago, one of the Group Africa companies ran a television mechanism in rural areas, and experienced major competition in this market. The competition was aggressive and intensive, and was an offshoot of one of South Africa's major publishing houses. In other words, they were much bigger and armed with far more resources – financial and other – than Group Africa could muster. Besides the many classic business tactics employed to block the company's entry, another dimension was added to our response.

Group Africa has a powerful *seriti/isithunzi* that has developed through our history. We are proud to be Africans and the *seriti/isithunzi* of our famous national ancestors adds to our own. *Seriti/isithunzi* became a major weapon in our hands. It was used to remind our clients of the great depth, professionalism and input they received when dealing with Group Africa. It was also used to close ranks in our own team and to give a clear picture of what they were fighting for, not only against. To achieve this, there were many discussions about the courage, fortitude and difficulties our warrior ancestors had experienced. As Africans, we were able to draw on our history. This added to our pride and our motivation to defend our turf.

Over an 18-month period, the competitor spent a lot of money, effort and time trying to break into this sector, but they failed dismally and no longer exist. However, Group Africa's *isithunzi* was enhanced. Tested in battle, the warrior prevailed.

The warrior ethic

One of the important pillars on which society, values and leadership are formed, is the 'warrior' and the discipline, self-control and tenacity he represents. We need to consider the African warrior, his frame of reference, his values and his environment.

When we talk of the development of a man's life, we are able to draw on a range of psychological and cultural imagery. We talk about puberty, adolescence and adulthood, about the forties' crisis and male menopause.

We know that in the development of a teenager, the youngster is likely to have skirmishes with other boys as he tests himself and is tested. As he gets older, he will directly or indirectly be involved in playground and, later, bar fights and challenges. Sophisticated as we are, we counsel against such behaviour. It is considered uncontrolled and unacceptable. Things can get nasty very quickly and out will come the knives or bottles, even guns! But something that is not easily understood seems to urge the warrior in him to test himself and his courage.

For hundreds of years, the Knights of Bushido[†] and the Samurai (the warrior class), have represented the honour and institutionalized morality of Japan – the discipline and the gentleness of those who have great physical and mental power. There is clear control and order, and with that comes respect. It is not something every Japanese person consciously aspires to, yet it affects everyone in Japan. This warrior culture has been harnessed to form the basis of one of the most powerful economies in the world. Every citizen is warrior-like in his discipline, loyalty and respect. Even the martial arts teach restraint.

Like a reflection of King Arthur and his Knights of the Round Table, the modern Western warriors can be seen in a boardroom. Take, for example, a board of directors. In the boardroom there is always a clearly perceived hierarchy which need not be stated. Over the years, the board will have been tested, there will have

---

[†] Code of honour and morality evolved by Japanese military knights.

been skirmishes between the members as the pecking order was established. There will have been fights between this board and other groups. The *seriti/isithunzi* of each member will have been established and in its powerful, invisible way, it creates a hierarchy on the board. The junior board members slowly learn the skills required and begin to position for power. The individuals compete with each other and are part of a team. They are totally interdependent.

We can talk about the capabilities of the Japanese with their discipline, order and respect, based on their warrior forebears. We can talk of the capabilities of Western businessman – also based on discipline, order and respect. But where do we explore this in Africa?

Africa has its warriors and the warrior ethic runs deep. It may have been smothered and hidden through the ravages of colonialism and apartheid, but it is still very much alive. For example, the Pedi warrior ethic is clearly the basis on which general leadership is established, even among very young people.

During the period immediately before initiation the young boys who will attend the session form a 'court' of their own, presided over by their leader (nKgwete) *who was chosen during their fight with switches. He is assisted as advisers by some other boys who emerged markedly during the fighting.*

– HO MONING, *The Pedi*

The stages of leadership development and the warrior are referred to in terms of cattle. In Africa, enormous importance is attached to cattle and the various characteristics that different animals reflect. In all cattle-based societies these characteristics are used in vivid imagery to define and describe different stages in the development of a man. An ox is seen as gentle, compliant, co-operative and social. For example, oxen will work as a team pulling the yokes of a plough or cart. The bull is seen as aggressive, violent, assertive, competitive, anti-social and with *inhliziyo emphi* (an ugly heart). It displays extreme individuality.

There are clear existential categories in the development of a male[†].

Creation of the warrior hero (bull/*inkunzi*)

Umfana	boy
Iqwele	senior boy
Ibhungu	adolescent warrior
Insizwa	warrior

[†] This is an outline of Zulu development. However, I wish to emphasize that this ethic and structure is paralleled in all other cattle-based societies. For example, among the Xhosa, from a young boy *(umntwana)* to a revered elder *(isinyanya)*, the full progression is: *umntwana, intwana, inkwenkwe, umkweta, ikrwala, umfana, ikhaba, liqina, yindoda, yingwevu, inkonde, isinyanya*. Among the Maasai, a boy *(enkayioni)* progresses through circumcision as *olbarnoti*, and the warrior *(ilmoran)*, into the stage of elderhood *(ilmoruak, olpayne, iltasati)*.

Taming of the warrior hero (ox/*inkabi*)

Umnumzana	homestead head
Ikheka	senior head
Izeku	senior elder

From this model it can be seen that, in the words of Johny Clegg, 'a man spends much of his life creating himself as a warrior, only to spend the rest of his life trying to tame the warrior that he created'.

A young boy has a reasonably peaceful and uncomplicated life until he reaches the age of about seven or eight. At this time, he enters the stick-fighting fraternity, first fighting with leafy branches and then with real weapons. This is the start of the development of his courage, skill and the ability to exert key values in the warrior system – such as *inkani* (stubborn determination) and *ukuzimisela* (complete preparedness). These values are seen as extremely important in the development of a male.

The male condition, which is modelled on the bull, has to be constantly marshalled, cajoled and controlled to avoid anti-socialism. But there is something in the warrior that resists this, which can be seen physically. When the warrior captain says, for example, 'It's time to go', the warrior will not move. This would be too compliant. The warrior captain will have to cajole, pressure and lead superbly to get his 'bulls' to move. The view is simple: only through earned respect can one man lead another. No man can be forced to listen to or respect another.

At every wedding and coming-of-age, young boys are forced by older boys to fight. This is not a playground; it is real and has a clear purpose. Boys will fight their best friends as a way of testing their friendship. In this way, they learn to trust each other in preparation for a time when, as a group or clan, they may have to fight another group.

This makes the boys stand apart as individuals – as young bulls. They gradually realize they will always be lonely (even within the camaraderie of the group) and it is often a traumatic revelation. This is similar to the realization that often strikes senior management in business: leadership is lonely. These young men are already learning the crucial leadership lesson: to be self-reliant and to thoroughly test those on whom they may have to rely. By the time a boy is around 14 years old and about to become a senior boy, he will have fought everyone in his group. The pecking order will have been established and be very strong.

The *insizwa* (warrior) is at his full potential at around 30 to 35 years. As a warrior, he is constantly challenging and being challenged at stick-fights and dances. The stick-fights are not seen by the community, as they reveal the pecking order. They occur in the veld, away from the ceremonies.

If you have had the good fortune to experience a traditional Zulu wedding *(indwendwe)* you will have shared the joy of one of life's celebrations. No invitations are sent, just the knowledge that there is to be a wedding. Those who wish to share in this moment arrive. Normally it involves the entire community. Joyous singing and ululating, ancient dances and mock fighting by lone warriors as they *giya*[†]; brightly coloured *ibaye* (wraps) cover the shoulders, and the married women wear *indlokos* (headdresses), beautiful beaded necklaces and soft leather aprons. Rank upon rank of young maidens dance gentle steps together as one, as if they lived many centuries ago when their ancestors danced these same dances. Powerful men bear sticks and shields. *Ibutho* (regiment) after *ibutho* arrive. Family groups sing over the sound of existing celebration and song. The old women ululating and waving branches of green leaves, stagger tiredly back and forth, ahead of the girls and young men. An ordered mass of humanity sways back and forth, doing different steps to the same beat.

Then there is a powerful call from a lone voice – fast, staccato. There is unified response from the men, sitting up expectantly, calling. Another lone call. Suddenly, hands are being clapped as if to a drum, a blood-stirring chant, powerful voices. Unity. A lone man appears, flaying sticks and a shield about him. Imaginary enemies. A great 'fight', a great warrior, a great *giya*. It is a celebration of life and masculinity. Ululating women rush around him, clear of the whistling sticks. They encourage, tease and challenge, but he struts off to one side, unconcerned, as if alone and as if nothing has happened. The women dance.

There is a rush from one side by the *amaqhikazi,* the young engaged girls. They are brash, bold, beautiful, warrior-like and powerful. With pebbles in cans tied to their ankles they perform strange jumps and off-beat steps. Together they defy protocol and the world. They are 'in-between' people as they are neither unattached virgins nor married women. They are loners grouped together in a rite of passage. A wedding is an amazing thing!

Then there is the bridal party, with the dignified matron's dances, the veil and the knife, which symbolically cuts off the past. The bride approaches her husband among the warriors, then turns back to the women. There is more *giya,* more dance, more song, and more people arrive.

Then the sun is low in the west and all is quiet. Old men sit in the shade drinking beer in *izinkhamba* (clay pots), and traditional brews and Lion quarts in bottles. The married women, noble and dignified, laugh and joke together. Suddenly moved to song, they burst forth and another dance ensues. Young warriors and girls gradually drift off.

On the ridge above the *umuzi* (homestead), where the wedding takes place, another gathering occurs. To the uninitiated, what one sees here will appear to be rampant violence. But it is a celebration of masculinity and life; a time for the warriors and a joyous test.

Initially great lines of warriors will spar with one another. It is all extremely disciplined and ordered, controlled with great charisma and exceptional leadership

---

[†] To metaphorically fight imaginary enemies; something akin to a *kata* in karate.

by the warrior captains. Then the real challenges start with young warriors intent on moving up the pecking order. There is a sudden quiet. A circle of men and two young gladiators become framed by the blurring of the whistling sticks. *Nayi inkunzi!* (Here is the bull!)

Should one man fall or falter, the warrior captains immediately stop the fight. It is customary once the tension has subsided after the fight, for the victor to bathe or bind the wounds of his opponent, openly demonstrating that he holds no malice. The fight was the fight and there it shall remain, even though it may be remembered and celebrated in the victor's praise poem. The two antagonists may well be great friends. This fight will, through its very greatness, increase the status, the *isithunzi*, of these men.

The *ugoso* (warrior captain) will try to reduce the internal conflict experienced by all the men through praise poetry and song. Never denying the tension, they sing songs of their status as bulls. But they also sing of how nice it would be if they could be friends, all the while knowing that, as bulls, this can never be.

But now the warrior has to stop all of this. He marries, becomes a provider, and a source rather than a taker of life. He attends elders' meetings, explores the law and begins to control young warriors. This is an extremely stressful period of change (not unlike the change South Africa as a nation experienced during 1994 and 1995). The dynamic tension of this life-changing period between the *insizwa* and the *umnumzana* is once again seen in the imagery of cattle: the bull can either be the seed line or be castrated to become an ox *(inkabi)*. An old ox is called *inxahi*, but that is all he is: an old ox. The bull, however, first becomes an adult bull *(inkunzi)*, and if he is not tamed, he becomes 'one who lives alone', wild, like a buffalo. The nobility of this state is greatly respected. These men are called *ishinga*.

The important feature of the warrior ethic and developmental structure is how it interprets into everyday life. The young warrior no longer goes to war or raids cattle. He becomes a migrant worker and earns money (his symbolic herd of cattle). The clans of the cattle-based societies in the south (Swazi, Tsonga, Sotho, Zulu, Bhaca, Pondo, Mfengu, Xhosa) and in East Africa (Maasai, Turkana, Samburu, Rendille and Pokot, to mention a few) are constantly testing themselves. Incidentally, in East Africa, cattle-raiding is still a feature of life as an *ilmoran* (warrior). In South Africa this converts into faction-fighting where the opportunity exists to use an AK47. However, most men choose to reflect their honour and courage in the traditional way.

This ethic is not limited to Africa. In the east, martial arts are a recognized expression of inner discipline. They are also violent. To be martial reflects a fondness of fighting. But it is not only the fight itself that is important. It is the symbolic capital gained by successfully adhering to the warrior ethic of stubborn determination and complete preparedness, and the inner discipline that comes with courage.

The fighting ethic translates into different forms, one of which is dance. The stick-fighting is real, violent confrontation. Then there is a shadow – a ritual display. Finally, there is dance *(gida)* which is a metaphoric elaboration of the fight. All of the features of the stick-fight are present in the dance. The regimentation, the individuality, the rugged determination, the challenge, the constant striving to move up the pecking order. In all of this there is order, structure and discipline. There is an intrinsic drive, a passion to improve, and an understanding and acceptance that the individual and the team are crucial to life.

The young men are fully aware of one another as people. They are quickly able to differentiate between a leader who has *isithunzi* or *seriti* and one who does not. It is in this difficult and highly individualized environment that leadership expresses itself through combinations of consensus and powerful *isithunzi*.

At a dance, when two men challenge each other with meaning, it is fascinating to observe the dynamic of leadership that emerges. Recognizing the power and danger of the challenge, the *ugoso* will normally stop the dance and create new structures to deal with the new circumstance. This will involve the watching community from which up to three 'judges' will be drawn. These people will be seated directly in front of the dance group and separated from the community, thereby ensuring they are not influenced by onlookers.

It is only once the judges are in place that the *ugoso* directs his attention back to his group. Now he goes through elaborate preparation: cajoling the young men to sing louder, slapping this one back into the group, whipping that one lightly with the thong of his whistle for not clapping. Only once the dynamic tension is re-established in the group – only once there is a tangible aura – does he allow the dance to be opened by a 'non-combatant'. This will be done quickly and powerfully by a senior dancer.

Now the challengers begin, one at a time and one after the other. Initially there is intricate and fancy footwork, delicate steps, then high kicking and double kicking on the same leg. Slowly they both begin to tire and the battle changes from one of skilful finesse to one of rugged endurance. And still they dance while the judges sit impassively.

The *ugoso* stays well clear of the dancers now, working only with the rest of the group who sing and clap. Eventually, one of the dancers stumbles and suddenly it is over. The *ugoso* whistles and the group stops its support. The judges confer and call the *ugoso*, who listens respectfully to their verdict. But the result is clear to everybody. Even so, the *ugoso* returns to the group, starts a song and a rhythm, and drags the victor out to dance once more. When he has done this, he encourages the victor to draw the loser out to dance. In so doing, the victor demonstrates there is no malice, and he allows the loser to dance the final round alone. He allows him his dignity, and this is akin to bathing an opponent's wounds after a stick fight. All of this is very carefully, delicately and interactively led by the *ugoso*, by reading the nuance of the group.

The men demand strong leadership, and this translates to other areas of their lives: to the workplace, to schools, to the soccer club, etc. In all of these areas there is great frustration in disciplining and controlling young men. But it is a leadership challenge with great rewards, as one works with the very essence of the warrior. Is it right to 'castrate' these young bulls simply to force them to conform? Or does one harness this amazing energy as a life-force to be encouraged and nurtured? Although this relates overtly to men, as Bushido in Japan, the entire society is affected by the values and the power of the warrior ethic and the discipline it demands.

We saw a very strange thing, we were sitting, my wife and I, outside a hotel; we were enjoying the distant sights of the city of Osaka. We saw a man and a woman come towards us, along the concreted riverbank and then we saw these people take off their clothes and then go into the river. They never came out and we later learnt to our surprise that these people were dead. They had thrown themselves gently into the river and why? Because the man had been five minutes late at his job. I was most astonished. It was to be one of several strange things I was to see in that faraway land. A man so filled with shame, taking his own life and that of his wife because he had been late at work. But this is the Japanese way.

– Credo Mutwa

Likewise, the African warriors, founded on the values already discussed, make amazing, strong, wise and sensitive workers and leaders. By being encouraged to nurture their own cultural approach to life and leadership, and not to dismiss it in favour of westernization, these men and Africa can become truly empowered.

So, if you put an overall on the warrior, the warrior is the worker. The worker must come to work at the right time in order to fight as much battle as he can in the shortest possible time. He must fight it well – that is the way of the warrior. The warrior must not come to battle full of anger but he should be full of inspiration. When he faces a problem on the battlefield he must ask the chief or the general or the induna for help. But sometimes he must act on his own. But in acting on his own, he must be careful that he does not destabilize the rest of the impis *(regiments or teams).*

– Credo Mutwa

It is rather ironic that Africans fought against colonialism to retain the integrity of their African-ness. But, now that is gone, they struggle just as desperately to unload any vestiges of African-ness to emulate Americans or Europeans.

The African warrior is exactly that: African. Where the warrior ethic has faded, I believe it needs to be actively and purposely re-established among our people. For it is from this base that productivity can rocket, and that efficiencies and effectiveness in all fields can be grown. We deal here with a culture of tenacity. Should we destroy it completely, we will be lost. The African warrior ethic gives us a foundation of discipline, just as the Samurai have done for Japan. Without it, and coupled with the breakdown of traditional community structures, there is great danger of a complete loss of discipline, drive, community and team, and there will be no pride.

We know now of the powerful drives of the warrior and his formation as a man (the individual), of *ubuntu* and its compassion, humanity and care (the community). And we know of *seriti/isithunzi*, our inner shadow growing as we do good deeds (the life-force).

In a strong community there is a fine balance between self-actualization (individual), survival (dependency on the community) and the interaction between the two (the life-force: a comfortable linking of the warrior, *ubuntu* and *seriti/isithunzi*). Even though the warrior appears extremely individualistic, he is not in conflict with the community. As part of the clan, he understands the importance of family and the need to stand united. He lives *ubuntu* and community. As a warrior and as part of the clan, he understands *seriti/isithunzi* and is driven to enhance his own and his family's.

The concepts of warriorhood, *ubuntu* and *seriti* are not only rural phenomena. The expression of these concepts in rural traditional areas is obviously different from the way they are expressed in the cities, but they run throughout our societal structures. In a national survey conducted by Group Africa in 1995, of 1 637 people representing all African language groups, both urban and rural, 41 per cent indicated that stick-fighting had formed an integral part of their development. For the rest, the echo of the warrior affects them as does the echo of chivalry for Western men now placed in a society where sexual equality theoretically displaces it.

Some 50 per cent to 60 per cent of South Africa's population lives in rural areas and is still very much in tune with traditional cultures. All the transitional communities (those living in informal areas) in the cities are often filled with people who have recently moved from rural areas. They, too, are very much in tune with their culture. Of course, this is not to say they wear traditional clothing and live in wattle-and-daub huts. It is how the people think that really matters.

Tribal leadership

If we pursue a synergy between our own leadership in Africa and African people, it is crucial that the general features of traditional African leadership are recognized and incorporated in our thinking. This can be converted to other applications, in the workplace and in government.

Traditionally, the king represented the unity of the tribe and was the personification of the law. In other words, his example was expected to be exemplary. This is now the expectation of all leadership, be it in business or elsewhere. Any questions or disputes about the law were settled by discussion among the old and wise elders of the tribe. The chief's councillors represented the people and it was their consensus that defined the laws.

He [the chief] is not expected to partake in the discussion of the case, but merely judges when it has been sufficiently discussed and when a majority opinion becomes apparent, at which stage he 'cuts' the case and gives his verdict accordingly.
— HO Moning, *The Pedi*

Since everyone is at liberty to express his opinions freely at court, the case often drags on for a long time. But this system has the advantage of indicating, to the headman in charge, in what direction the preponderance of opinion lies among those who have attended the trial. Then, when the headman feels that the case has been sufficiently discussed, he calls for order and pronounces his judgement, which is invariably the opinion of the court.
— EJ Krige, *The Social System of the Zulus*

Although the Zulu king was assumed to be proprietor of everything, people, land and cattle, he could neither legislate, make war, nor allot land without the consent of the tribal council... Thus in giving out laws without this consent, he would be departing from custom and obedience would depend on public opinion.
— EJ Krige, *The Social System of the Zulus*

It is important to point out that it was accepted that there was a collective responsibility to uphold the law. If an individual saw a wrong being done and did nothing to stop it, or did not report it, then that individual incurred responsibility for the act. Taking cognizance of the attitude towards community and collective responsibility meant that anyone present at a case could question the involved parties. Such a court was called *inkundla* by the Xhosa people. The only person excluded here was the presiding headman as his role was to ensure order and procedure were maintained, to sum up, and to pass final judgement.

All adult men are entitled to attend the court of the chief and although attendance is not compulsory, it is expected that men attend these hearings as often as possible. All men in attendance are allowed to partake in the deliberations, although the elders do not regard with favour young men of little experience or knowledge of the law who address the court, and will silence them unless they are involved in the case.
— HO Moning, *The Pedi*

Traditional African leadership includes several features, some of which are indicated below:
▲ The chief personifies the unity of the tribe. He must 'live' the values of his community and be an exemplary model to his people.

▲ The chief is not an autocrat, and must rely on councillors representing the people to assist him.

▲ The chief must be guided by consensus. If he is not, the people will ignore his decision or his 'law'.

▲ The people must always be strongly represented and the entire (adult) community should attend court or 'hearings'.

▲ The people have a responsibility to each other, and collectively, to ensure the laws (values) are upheld.

▲ Because of the collective responsibility, everyone has the right to question in an open court.

▲ The concept of openness is an important value, recognizing that retribution is not possible for something said in a correct and open 'court' forum.

▲▲▲▲

CHAPTER 5

Conflict and confusion in tribe, First World and Third World

Arican culture has generally been seen in derogatory, 'banana republic' terms as something unacceptable, incompetent and usually bankrupt: 'Africa is a basket case.' This is mainly due to the confusion that exists over what African culture actually is. In most instances, the African way is seen as ill-disciplined, corrupt, lethargic, unproductive and inefficient.

This is not a true reflection of African culture. Rather, it is a Western view of the African way, which is based on a society bastardized and destroyed by colonialism. Unfortunately, this view is not totally wrong, but the terminology is wrong. African tribal society and standards must not be confused with the lost middle ground. The fundamental difference between this element of the Third World and First World or tribal society is discipline.

In discussing Third World people, we need to be clear on definitions and points of reference. A First World country is a 'developed' country. A Third World country is one which is 'developing'. Classically, the term 'Third World' has to do with economics, infrastructure limitations and needs. It is also linked with massive population growth, poor education and health care, and shortages of all types of skilled labour and profession.

But who are the people in these societies? The Zulu people identify three distinct groups:

Amabhinca	Those who are traditionalists remaining very close to their tribal way.
Amakholwa	Those who follow Western ideologies and who are mostly Christian.
Amagxagxa	Those who borrow from both of the previous groups. They are

somewhere in a cross-over cultural zone, are neo-traditionalists, and make up by far the largest group.

Among the Amakholwa, in particular, there are people who are very opposed to traditionalism, seeing it as pagan, savage and contemptible. For them, their religion gives them the discipline and integrity so easily lost when tribal groupings break down. They have very high moral standing and some groups, such as the Shembe and Zionist churches, even disallow the use of cigarettes and alcohol. These people are in the cross-over zone of the Third World, but they retain their dignity and their discipline. In areas in which traditionalism has disappeared, the societies often find replacement structures and remain cohesive, with great integrity and moral fibre. The values of the group win through.

But there is a dark and utterly destructive cloud to the Third World: a massive movement of individuals turning their backs on their traditions and discipline and, in so doing, the closeness of community and *ubuntu*. They replace it, not with the best of the First World, but often with the very worst. They are self-serving and care nothing for the community other than what it can deliver to them personally. They seek to take, not to give or share. Many of these people have managed to educate themselves very well. They know how to manipulate Westerners and how to use, to their own ends, their once-upon-a-time tribe. They are part of the Third World but they also exist in the First World. We shall call this group the 'Takers'. Takers have neither integrity nor discipline. They serve the dollar-god of power and will do anything for it. Unfortunately, the tribal way has become confused with Takers, so let's explore these sectors and disentangle them.

In both First World and tribal societies, a strong social fabric of culture, control and discipline is apparent. Social norms, rites, ethics and traditions exist and these form the foundation, or the core around which everything else revolves. First World societies have developed a fairly clear universal culture that supersedes language and tribe. Values such as honesty, majority rule, democracy, hard work, cleanliness, good manners, care, environmental concern, respect, justice, human rights, tolerance and strong democratic government are all generally accepted. These values form the culture. Discipline is a feature of all First World societies.

Tribal societies are also ordered, cultured and disciplined. However, in First World terms, they are economically poverty-stricken. But it can be argued that, in many respects, tribal societies are socially and morally extremely wealthy, for they have, as part of them, their philosophies in which all people share in the common good. They have absolute clarity on the structure and order of their society and they retain a deep and sincere care for the community, which is a noble domain worth far more than material riches.

First World people worldwide have gone beyond the efficiency and science of their racy business and professional lives in search of self. Books such as M Scott Peck's *The Road Less Travelled*, Stephen Covey's *The Seven Habits of Highly Effec-*

tive People and *Principle Centred Leadership* all explore deeply personal issues: issues of happiness. Isn't it amazing that almost everything in life has to do with emotion, yet nowhere in our schooling are we taught how to share feelings? Once we leave school we are encouraged, by business in particular, to be hard, macho and unfeeling. How often do we see a managing director weeping when the time comes to retrench a section of the workforce? Does he really feel nothing? Or is it simply conditioning that has taught him not to show his feelings?

Tribal people are still spontaneous and honest – especially when it comes to emotions. Their life views are deep and sincere. Just look at the ever-increasing interest of Americans, Europeans and the Japanese in the lost cultures of the Native American Indians. Only now that these cultures have practically disappeared are people realizing what they were and what wisdom they had.

In the past, 'the downside (was) always pointed out and never the beauty of our culture' says Roland Neiss, member of the Rosebud Sioux Tribal Council and director of the Alliance of Tribal Tourism (*The Star:* 18 March 1995). Now, of course, things have changed, and more and more people want to learn about and from the ancient ways.

It is my contention that from the point of view of ethics and values, or 'social morality', tribal and First World societies are almost identical, especially regarding the inner discipline of people. Even in issues like conservation, tribal peoples have shared what is now considered as an extremely advanced First World way of thinking. They saw themselves as custodians, realizing that if they destroyed the environment they could not survive. It appears that as we grow in wisdom in the First World, so we learn to respect the wisdom of the ancients. This wisdom still lives in tribal societies.

During the colonial era it was colonists who, through mechanisms such as missions and schools oriented to the Western way, began the destruction of tribal societies. The white world seemed hell-bent on making black Africa white. White values and white beliefs were vigorously pursued. The tribal societies were not respected in their own right and they were dismantled. They were disfigured by the new messages and they became ill – part new world, part old world – and, in this way, not whole.

To expect disfigured Africa and her Takers to respond to First World values, ethics and disciplines is ludicrous. The Third World Takers have no discipline. Why have billions of US dollars been siphoned off into secret Swiss bank accounts by leaders in Africa? Why has aid money disappeared? Why has famine relief been sold for personal gain? This is what Graham Hancock had to say in his powerful book, *Lords of Poverty*, about aid money channelled to help in economic adjustment programmes in the Third World:

...Corrupt Ministers of Finance and dictatorial presidents from Asia, Africa and Latin America are tripping over their own expensive footwear in their seemly haste to 'get

adjusted'. For such people money has probably never been easier to obtain than it is today: with no complicated projects to administer and no messy accounts to keep, the venal, the cruel and the ugly are laughing literally all the way to the bank. For them structural adjustment is like a dream come true. No sacrifices are demanded of them personally. All they have to do – amazing but true – is 'screw the poor', and they've already had plenty of practice at that.

– GRAHAM HANCOCK, *Lords of Poverty*

Graham Hancock's research also tells us that in, for example, a country like Zaïre, President Mobuto Sese Seko owns 51 Mercedes-Benz motor cars, 11 châteaux in Belgium and France, and a beachside villa on the Costa del Sol. Yet recently, 7 000 teachers were dismissed for budgetary reasons. The country is ranked as the eighth poorest nation on earth and the life expectancy for the average citizen in 1987 was just over 50 years. Yet Mobuto Sese Seko has become one of the world's wealthiest men. His personal assets, mostly beyond the borders of Zaïre, are estimated by Western intelligence sources at between $3- and $4-billion.

The President has achieved wealth on this scale by the simple expedient of stealing it. According to Erwin Blumenthal, a German banker sent to Zaïre by the IMF [International Monetary Fund], 18% of the national budget is routinely earmarked for Mobutu's personal use.

– GRAHAM HANCOCK, *Lords of Poverty*

In December 1977, Central African Republic President Jean Bedel Bokassa spent $20-million out of a total annual amount of $38-million in aid from France. The reason? A glittering, if vulgar, ceremony transforming him from a president to an emperor. He wore a crown worth $2-million and robes that cost $145 000. All of this happened in what was, at the time, Africa's poorest country.

In Uganda in 1985, Dr Mahmood Mamdani, associate professor of science at Uganda's Makerere University, called on Western aid donors to review the nature of the projects they were financing. It was clear, he said, that they were in no way benefiting the poor but only increasing the riches of the already rich. For this 'subversive' criticism, he was deprived of his Ugandan citizenship by then President Milton Obote.

Why have there been so many one-party states and coup after coup? The reason is that, in the past, many African leaders have been totally and unapologetically self-serving. Yet the First World does not view Africa as different from itself for fear of discrimination. It is fundamentally different because Third World Africa, which is led largely by Takers, has no discipline. It is not governed according to the same ethics and values as either the First World or the tribal world, and therefore does not respond to them.

It is the blatant rape of these fragile societies by fellow Africans that makes the issue even more repugnant. The Third World Takers are far more insidious and warped than the colonials ever were, yet this is exactly the behaviour and attitude for which colonial settlers were criticized and expelled. The Takers obviously learnt their appalling, self-serving lessons well!

Cleverly corrupt African leaders have learnt to tell the First World that First World demands are 'not in tune with the culture of Africa', and, because of this, First World leaders back off. Third World Takers use their race to blackmail the First World. It must not be blackmailed. If the principle is just, and if they are truly non-racial people, the First World must ignore the threats of blackmail. One can be tribal and not discriminate racially. The principle that provides for this is equal rights. This does not exclude the fact that people are different – as are men and women, or the Scottish and the English – but both should be treated equally.

Third World Taker leaders clearly laud the materialism of the First World. But tribal leaders are more wary, perhaps due to the perceived lack of community in the First World, or its apparent shallowness and materialism. An interesting, if rather literal, tribal view of First World materialism and status is found in Alistair Graham and Peter Beard's fascinating book, *Eyelids of Morning*. A research team working with crocodiles in Lake Turkana in Northern Kenya had this to say:

So it was one day Johnson, his wife Osa and Vern the pilot landed on Fergusons Gulf at Kalakol. They waited with interest to see the reaction of these people who had never seen an 'aero' before. The Turkana reacted with shrieks of laughter – directed not at the flying machine but at the funny Americans. Such comical fellows! They virtually ignored the aircraft.

Piqued, Johnson thought perhaps they hadn't fully comprehended the nature of the beast. Accordingly he asked Vern to fly the plane off the water and put it down again, this time on land, a manoeuvre that would surely confound them. But as the craft circled above them, 'they only smiled as if to humour me'. This time the plane, having rolled to a stop, did attract attention. The Turkana noticed that the wings made a tempting band of shade over the scorching sand, in which an exasperating crowd promptly settled.

They had one more try. Vern took one of the men for a flip but on their return he stepped out as if nothing whatsoever had happened and sat down again to enjoy the shade of the wings. Before leaving, Johnson asked an old man if he would like to possess a plane of his own. No, the old man replied, he certainly would not; whoever heard of a Turkana making a fool of himself in a flying machine?

Clearly, these Turkana people, like all tribal people, know exactly what they are and what they are not. Their sense of self-esteem, well developed and completely intact, has no need to go chasing after First World toys. They have their own way of life and they have community.

However, Africa is dominated by the proliferation of Third World Takers and, because of this, it is corrupt. Remember, we must not confuse tribal Africa with the Takers, and we must not allow such leaders to tell us that they are tribal or traditional. They are not. They simply use the tribe to gain their own political ends; they want power, wealth and status, at any cost. The cost is mostly that of the people, the poor humble people who till the lands and work the factories, who dig in the mines and fix the roads. The colonials did the same. Africa needs to move away from this, to create a new way to regain its dignity and, above all, its discipline and pride.

Which way should Africa move? Into the First World, discarding its cultural heritage in favour of hamburgers and French fries and other Americanisms? Or into its tribal roots? Or the way of the Third World Takers? In fact, we do not have to choose. We can have tribal and First World features at the same time. And this would not be a first-time occurrence in the world.

An excellent example of such a group is found in the Jews. Their culture has survived thousands of years of savaging. Their tribe was scattered across all the nations of the world, but they still managed to become First World and remain true to their Jewish culture. They never discarded their culture in favour of development, and, even under immense pressure to hide from it, they still carried it with them.

We must ensure that our history and our culture are carried with us into the new African First World way. Without that we have nothing, and we will continue to slide towards anarchy and oblivion. A society without a living history, heritage and pride is a non-society. We must reach out to our ancestors.

This is not new to the world. In 1941, Mao Tse Tung, when talking of returning Chinese students and intellectuals said:

…but about their own ancestors they have to apologize and say they've forgotten. They are not ashamed but proud when they understand very little or nothing about their own history… Many are ignorant of anything which is their own, yet hold on to Greek and foreign tales…

– S SCHRAM, *Mao Tse-Tung*

Amazingly, South Africa is somehow weathering the storm. The appalling damage that was done by apartheid is, ironically, balanced by the relatively high level of education of its senior people. Apartheid forced our best people into exile, prison or leadership roles, where they were forced to take a stand and grow. Our leaders studied and were educated in exile and in jail. The greatest weapon that could be used against the system was education and knowledge. This educational thrust drove us towards the First World. Simultaneously, in order to survive in the poverty-stricken homelands, our tribal people grew strong. The culture of generations was stimulated, even if its overt expression in tribal dress and building design waned. The traditional ways and values of the past persisted because they were the only firm point in people's otherwise chaotic lives.

There has been a dual positive development, the stronger of which has been the First World thrust. However, the Third World Taker culture threatens and grows as long as we remain poor and have no work. Culture leads in every way. Right now, we are in a position where we can make decisions about our culture and the form it should take. South Africa is the Rainbow Nation. We should celebrate our differences and grow from this unnatural birth into a powerful and productive nation.

PART 2

CHAPTER 6

▲▲▲▲

What we are

Recently, I ran a leadership team-building exercise in which a group of leaders were tasked with moving to a series of points plotted on a map. Different groups started at different places at the same time and knew about one another. Although the execise was never meant to be a race, the participants turned it into one.

The obvious starting point in this exercise is to establish where one is on the map. By knowing that, one can plan the best route possible, taking into account the mountain of equipment and baggage that has to be carried, and the fitness level of the team members. Yet, in team after team, people rush to find a short-cut, asking passersby about their destination. They ask a range of questions designed to help them locate their objective without taking time to determine where they are! They start the vehicle, check the equipment and load the back-packs, but avoid the obvious question: Where are we now?

In pursuing our dreams we often lose sight of the same issue – passionately, sometimes desperately, but quite honestly challenging every ounce of energy into the charge to our goals. But we need to know where we are now before we can ever hope to reach our dreams.

The world is not static. Like culture and life, everything changes all the time. We need to keep plotting ourselves to ensure that we hit what we are aiming for. It is imperative to continually take stock of where we are in life, and to check ourselves and our businesses. The aim should be to creatively destroy ourselves and our businesses, frequently, so that each time we rebuild, it happens without the baggage and flaws of a model built for a different world. It takes a lot of courage to attack oneself. It is a painful experience, so we often make cursory gestures, attempting to bluff ourselves into believing that we have fully analysed ourselves and that everything is just fine.

If you ask a colleague or a leader how his business or life is shaping up, it is very seldom that you will be told about the flaws. They always appear to be 'motivat-ed', 'real professionals' or 'working like Trojans'. People seldom, if ever, talk of themselves as 'unqualified', 'struggling' or 'unethical'.

Many readers will think: Everything is going great, so why change? Is it really going great? Does everyone in your business or school or club think it's going great? Have you asked them? If you did, did you really listen and understand what you were being told? Let's dig a little deeper. Is your business completely clear of negativity, office politics and destructive inter-staff or inter-management conflict? These issues are symptomatic of far deeper problems which directly erode happiness and, therefore, productivity. If you are aware of just one of these issues in your business – beware! It is a symptom of the disease called conflict.

It is a psychological fact that people generally do not like change. We have to train ourselves to expect it and accept it. Most people, especially if they are comfortable, don't go chasing it. Ask yourself the following question and give yourself a moment to think about your answer: Am I happy and comfortable with the way things are?

Be specific. Ask it a few times and relate it to your job, your marriage, your career, your life. Pause and really think about these issues. What we are doing is something we will call 'roadmapping' from now on.

You may say that you are quite comfortable with your life. But if you are really honest with yourself, you are likely to find a few things that you know should change. Are you actively seeking to change them? Did you start with yourself when you analysed the situation? What are you doing that is causing these problems? You can decide on a course of action to change things, but first you have to be bold enough to really look at yourself. Ask yourself: Am I everything I would like to be? If you aren't (and I guess that includes most of us!), plot your current position very carefully and in detail. List all the things that are not good, either on paper or in your head. What you are doing is finding yourself on life's map. There are no shortcuts, no easier ways, and no models to make us feel comfortable. Only by doing this can we grow and move on. Do the same for your business. Don't list the good things – that's easy! Get down to the things you are not good at, the things you have done as a business or personally of which you are not very proud. Don't gloss over them – dig, analyse and understand what it is that you don't like. Tell yourself that you will not be like that ever again, then set the picture of what you don't want firmly aside.

The next step is to create a vivid picture in your mind of what you do want. Make it a very clear picture with lots of positive detail. Only once you have clearly plotted your current position on life's map, can you hope to get to the point you are aiming for.

Industrial relations

We are all aware that industrial relations deal with the relationships between workers and employers. Industrial action is taken by employees, in the form of strikes, work stoppages, and so on, in protest against a management action with which they do not agree.

This form of interaction has its roots in the Industrial Revolution, where workers were outrageously exploited and where the only recourse was collective bargaining with the employer. Trade unions are organized workers' associations formed specifically to protect and further their rights and interests.

Industrial relations are based on the premise of exploitation and conflict: 'them' and 'us'. 'They [the managers] are trying to exploit us for as much work and as little pay as possible.' Or, 'They [the workers] are trying to do as little as possible for unrealistic pay demands.' This is a Western concept of the worker-employer relationship that was imported directly from Europe. In the past, the worker has been exploited, but productivity levels have been appalling and wage demands have been excessive. Are we Europeans? There is absolutely no need for us to proceed along this path. This entire form of business interaction and negotiation is, I believe, obsolete. We should approach one another, not as enemies, but as allies in the fight against poverty, low productivity and exploitation. We should be allies in the fight for wealth-creation and happiness. If you truly have the interests of workers and sound business at heart, and if you wish to see a highly productive business community driving our nation and our continent into world leadership, read on.

African and Western work groups

Western management runs work groups and individuals in terms of role and function. 'Joe Ndlovu' is given a task or role. He understands exactly what his role and function is, and he is measured against this. It is an individually oriented approach to management. The African work group, however, assesses itself on moral and emotional grounds. Role and function, although important, are not primary concerns. In this work group there needs to be a superordinate goal for the collective to aspire to. Let's look at an example to illustrate both approaches.

In the Western environment, let's assume we are responsible for an enterprise which employs hundreds of people. It could be a factory, an advertising agency or a government office. Ben is a cleaner. He is middle-aged and has a bit of a lame leg; he is fairly friendly, but very quiet. However, he's not doing his job very well. One of his functions is to sweep all the passageways in the offices and he is simply not very good at it. He is spoken to casually by his manager but nothing changes, the floors remain poorly swept. Industrial relations procedures are followed, and he receives a verbal warning. Things don't change. He gets a written warning and still nothing changes. We give him a final written warning itemizing very clearly all the things he is not doing. We tell him that he has to accomplish certain standards by a certain date or he will have to leave. Nothing changes, Ben is given notice and told to leave the company.

No sooner has this happened, or we experience labour problems and are threatened with strike action to have Ben reinstated. We cannot believe it. We show the staff and union officials all the correspondence, all the warnings. We demonstrate that he was not performing against the standards we expect – that he was unsuccessful in both role and function. We have surly, unco-operative staff if they are not actually striking against 'unfair dismissal'. Western managers will all be asking each other, with no limit to their frustrations: What is wrong with these people?

There is a very important reason why the people are on strike and reacting as they are. They view this issue from a completely different perspective – through a different paradigm.

In the African work group there's a moral and emotional response to doing business. Here's Ben, the cleaner who sweeps the floor. Everybody in the factory environment, that community, knows that Ben is the sole breadwinner for his immediate family and for two other brothers' families who are unemployed. They know that he has a very sick wife and child, and that he is responsible for 10 or 12 people. You warn him that he's not doing very well. He tries to do better but he just can't. Why? Because of where he is forced to live. Due to the housing shortage, he has to travel a considerable distance to and from work. He gets up at 4 a.m. and gets home at 8 p.m. every day. He is exhausted and positioned for failure.

Rather than firing Ben, the African work group will be saying, 'Let's talk to him; let's find out what it is that's limiting him. If he can't do this work, surely it's our responsibility to keep him employed and to move him into a different environment where he will be useful, where he will be able to achieve for himself, for us, and to help him at home. We can't ignore the fact that he is supporting all those people.' What they are doing is pointing out that there's a moral and emotional connection – that it is not just role and function that are important.

Frequently there is conflict because this is not understood. This is not to say that the business is stuck with 'dead wood'. Once the group works together to improve the work output of an individual, and once a real human effort has been made to accommodate, train and grow a person, it will be accepted that, unless he improves, he will have to leave. If he doesn't improve, he will be putting another community at risk: the workers – the team that makes up the business.

For this community to understand productivity and that business is not a charity, considerable effort needs to be made in training. In other words, an amount of time equal to that spent by leaders trying to talk to their staff and understand the African work ethic should be spent educating the entire workforce in the nature of business and economics. Seen against world standards, there are some startling revelations. European companies spend around four per cent of their payroll on training and development. During 1994, only 0,05 per cent was spent on it in South Africa! No wonder we have difficulty understanding one another!

Tribe, ethnicity and the conflict within

The word 'tribe' conjures up a range of images: primitive savages and ancient rites, exotic tribal dress, smoke, drums and mystery. For some, tribes are fascinating, while for others, they are repulsive. Tribes, whether we like it or not, are not just entities that existed long ago. They exist now, not only in distant rural places, but in our hearts, for it is to the tribe that we retreat when we are most threatened.

Although Maslow's hierarchy of needs has been eclipsed by later theories of motivation, it is still one of the most widely discussed and well known. He believed that within every human being there exists a hierarchy of five needs. As each need is met, so the next one in the hierarchy dominates:

1. Physiological   Includes the need to satisfy hunger, thirst, shelter, sex and other physical bodily needs.

2. Safety   Includes security and protection from physical and emotional harm or distress.

3. Social   Includes affection, belonging, acceptance and friendship.

4. Esteem   Internal: self-respect, autonomy and achievement. External: status, recognition and attention.

5. Self-actualization   The drive to achieve one's potential. This includes growth and self-fulfilment.

Ethnicity/needs model

Maslow

Ethnicity

Self-actualization
Esteem
Social
Safety
Physiological

Low

High

Physiological and safety needs are equated with survival, so the closer one is to survival on Maslow's hierarchy, the higher one's ethnicity is likely to be. The further removed from survival, the lower one's ethnicity is likely to be. Let's look at an example. Play along with me as we go back in time...

In 1973, Moçambique was a focal point for holidaymakers from the Transvaal: Lourenço Marques, Laurentino beer, camping, fishing, LM prawns, wonderful hotels, magnificent beaches and island paradises. Imagine that you are Portuguese and living, as many generations of your family before you have done, over-looking the city of Lourenço Marques. Business is wonderful. Each weekend and every holiday, thousands of South Africans flock to your city and spend their money. You are doing a course towards a degree in philosophy for fun. Your family wants for nothing. Life is good. You are self-actualizing.

Then, in 1974, at the stroke of a pen, the Portuguese relinquish control of the colonies of Angola and Moçambique. For years, the Portuguese army, the one into which you were conscripted as a young man, had been fighting Frelimo in the bush. In just a few days, Frelimo is going to take over the government! Images of Mau Mau in Kenya, the slaughter of civilians, even nuns in the Congo, let alone what you saw as a soldier, rush to mind. You look at your wife and two daughters, and at your beautiful home, and you know what you have to do: get out. You have no foreign currency, no passports, and it is too late to try and get them. So you pack all the valuables you can into your car. You squeeze in granny and the rest of the family and, along with what looks like the entire white Portuguese population of Moçambique, make your way to the South African border at Koma-tipoort. Overnight, you are a refugee.

Where do you all go? Bez Valley[†]! And why to Bez Valley? Because suddenly you need the tribe. You need the extended Portuguese family to survive. For here, in this strange country, your Portuguese escudos[‡] mean nothing; you are unable to even speak the language. It doesn't matter that in Lourenço Marques you were a landowner and a successful businessman. Here you have nothing. In order to survive, first the extended family and then the tribe draws together. Your uncle speaks a little English and helps you to find a job. In crises you group together and find ways of helping each other because you all experience the same threat. Ethnicity is high.

With time, the community is educated in the local culture. You learn to speak English and you progress quickly in business terms. Over the years, you once again become a well-to-do, successful businessman. Your children are at good local schools, but when they finish high school you decide to move. You no longer live in Bez Valley, although you still have friends there. Now you live in Sandton, Randburg or Mondeor[†‡].

A basic progression along Maslow's hierarchy has occurred. Once again, the Portuguese businessman is self-actualizing. He has a Xhosa neighbour on the one side, and an Afrikaner on the other. Across the road there is an English couple. They all know one another and get along well. Ethnicity is low because there is no threat.

If a community comes under threat, there is an immediate psychological shift back to tribe. This happened among many communities in the period immedi-

---

[†] A Johannesburg suburb with a very high percentage Portuguese population.
[‡] The currency in Moçambique until independence from Portugal.
[†‡] Upper-middle class Johannesburg suburbs.

ately prior to South Africa's first democratic elections: the AWB[†], the Zulus, the English and the Jews. A quick check was casually done, just to establish where the community/tribe was, so that they could be contacted if the need arose; a check to get the tribe's perspective on the threat. The same thing occurred in business.

Hopefully, truly free and enlightened people do not choose to revert to tribe when under threat. But the reality is that, vortex-like, they are sucked into it whether they like it or not. The realities of the African environment do not allow us to deny tribalism, although some people do. This appears to be more prevalent among people recently removed from a traditional environment. For example, the young woman who lives in the city and whose grandparents are deeply traditional, is likely to be dismissive of tradition. The underlying reason for this is the belief that Western aspirations will not be met if traditions are maintained. As we discussed earlier, using the Jews as an example, it is possible to be fully First World and to still accept and understand the nobility of the tribe and the dignity that comes with it.

It is the context in which the tribe is seen that is important. If it is a support group or a way of life, there is no problem. But when ethnicity is used to fan hatred of other groups, evil is being done.

There is no point in denying that ethnicity exists. It simply does, whether one likes it or not. But it need not be negative. It can be the most inclusive, colourful, wonderful and positive thing. Rather than dividing us, our differences can be celebrated and shared. Tremendous joy can be derived in the discovery of variety.

Use and misuse of intellect, communication and behaviour

Intellectualism, communication and behaviour should be well balanced in everyone, but specifically in leaders. Intellect should not be insensitive or arrogant. Communication needs to be clear, and behaviour should be disciplined, controlled and dignified.

It is the cohesion and balance between these three aspects that largely constitute sophisticated First World and tribal behaviour. Ironically, these very issues can be easily twisted and abused, especially by Takers. They use intellectualism and miscommunication to deceive and to get away with bad behaviour. Let us look at how imbalances can occur in each of the three areas.

Intellectualism

To be intellectual is to pursue understanding, knowledge, wisdom and logic. But intellect is only one aspect of humanity – the others being the emotional, physical, spiritual and psychological capacities. All of these need to be balanced. Balance is, I believe, a natural thing of Africa, as it is of the East, and as it is gradually becoming a noble dream of the slowly self-actualizing First World.

[†] Afrikaner Weerstandsbeweging, an ultra-rightwing Afrikaner group.

As one progresses in the pursuit of intellectual wisdom, 'the more one realizes how little one knows'. Balanced human intellectual development will therefore also reflect humility. True wisdom transcends arrogance. Of course, one routinely meets intellectual snobs, but these unfortunate people, who are machine-like in their processing of logic, have lost something of their humanity. Like computers, they show no emotion – it can only be spoken about, analysed and interpreted in intellectual terms. There is no feeling.

One of the dangers of a rapidly developing Africa is that we lose sight of balance. In pursuit of being First World, of displaying the success of our progress away from the tribe, we can easily lose ourselves in intellectualization.

We are Africans! We are not Americans or Europeans. We are Africans. And yet, in a state of sad and sometimes aggressive ignorance, many black people have lost touch with their African roots. In many instances, they are more 'Western' and more 'intellectual' than apparently Western whites. Because of this, they are even more lost, for now it is they who intellectualize everything. They are desperately clinging to intellectualism so that they can find themselves. In reality, they are taking future generations down the same road that the West has discovered is the way to lose one's humanity. This is reflected in the great drives in search of self, humanity, emotion, community and success. One quick scan across the popular titles in a bookshop will verify this.

Contrary to popular belief, primal religions are today reviving in many parts of the world. The superior attitude, which spread European civilization over the globe, spurred on by Western Christianity and materialism, has been discredited in the twentieth century. Native faith-ways – scorned, forbidden, almost destroyed – reached their lowest point at the end of the nineteenth century. Their flame was extinguished. But today the disregard for the earth, for community, for spirituality, have brought the whole human enterprise into jeopardy. Arising like a phoenix from the ashes, tribal peoples are gathering again in their ceremonial circles, remembering discarded teachings, renewing the ancient ways.

– THE WORLD'S RELIGIONS

At this point, intellectuals will be looking for proof and asking the question: Where is the logic? Jesus was a carpenter; Mohammed a caravan leader who grew up in bitter poverty. Gandhi, Zoroaster, Confucius, Abraham, Buddha: Were they all intellectuals or did they strive to true human balance and expression? We need to be very careful of over-intellectualizing at the expense of true honesty and humanity.

Communication

Communication skills, especially verbal skills, are held in esteem by most people. In the African tribal way, this is taken to an extreme in the oral traditions of the people. How a person says something is considered just as important as what that person has to say. This may be interpreted into lengthy, flowery speeches, when the individual could have made the point succinctly and efficiently, but the presentation will be enjoyed for its colour. There is no judgement here. There are simply two paradigms at play: African and Western.

However, once again there is conflict, even blatant abuse of culture as people are educated and move away from the tribe. As we have already discussed, people strive to be regarded as First World. They may even position themselves as fully First World. Well educated, intelligent and lucid they may be, but when it comes to challenges, wordiness to the extreme is the norm. This wordiness usually wears down discussion until the principle is lost and the debate itself becomes the issue. This is an abrogation of the dignity once attached to oratory skills.

The principle must remain sacrosanct. Third World Takers often hide behind laborious wordiness and, in so doing, destroy real, honest communication.

Behaviour

Both tribal and First World people are bound by social etiquette, customs and norms. Adhering to these is considered polite. It is simply bad-mannered and ill-disciplined to break free of these norms. By ignoring these norms one demonstrates that one belongs to neither the tribal nor the First World group.

In its existing form, business is a Western, First World concept. Therefore, certain Western disciplines will, of necessity, be incumbent on all people who are part of a business. Time-keeping is one of these disciplines. The appalling discipline that is evident over this issue alone is an utter abrogation of respect. It is not a cultural issue! The people most guilty of this are often well-educated and, in many instances, leaders. This is true even in government circles. A minister may make an arrangement to attend a particular function and then, without informing the organizers, simply choose to go elsewhere. This is disrespectful, demeaning, indicates a lack of discipline and flames the fallacy of 'the culture of Africans is impossible when it comes to time'.

When experiencing conflict, typical Taker behaviour is simply to avoid confronting the problem. For example, if there is a major disagreement that needs to be sorted out between two leaders in public, the one (who is probably in the wrong) will agree to all the meetings to sort out the problem and then not arrive for the meeting. There will always be a rather weak excuse, but the fact is that this is avoidance. The attending party will bluster and complain, but nothing will solve the problem. Another meeting will be scheduled and the same thing will happen again. Very soon, the party who is attending will give up in disgust, at which time, the other person will suddenly reappear, as if nothing is wrong. This is blatant politicking and the behaviour here is clearly aimed at avoiding accountability.

The Takers act out roles in an environment that demands disciplined, mature behaviour and accountability. After all, they educated themselves to get there in the first place. But now that they are in place and have power, prestige and money, they flout the very rules that make up the fabric of society and business. In tribal society, this type of ill-discipline and disrespect would never be tolerated.

Historically, Schoon and McLuckie, two traders who visited Mzilikazi when he was at enKungwini, reported on trials in which ghastly sentences were meted out to those found guilty of crimes such as murder, treason, adultery, theft, cowardice, disobedience and negligence. One example is of a tribesman who attempted to rape a Ndebele woman. His ears and genital organs were sliced off and he was left to his fate at the outskirts of the royal kraal.

Behavioural ill-discipline has even affected President Mandela, when one of his ministers chose to be out of the country rather than attend a meeting which he had called. The message? I can do whatever I like; there are no rules when one has power; democracy means I do not have to be disciplined. Fortunately, the President's very sharp reaction (though not as extreme as Mzilikazi's!) left no doubt that this type of behaviour is unacceptable. In a position of leadership, with people looking to you be a mentor and guide, the only result of ignoring such irresponsible behaviour is eventual anarchy.

CHAPTER 7

▲▲▲▲

The law and justice

Justice is a sense of fairness – of doing what is right and moral. That very morality is defined by the values of the community and justice can be done by using values as a moral guide. Laws can be upheld, but justice may not be done if the laws are not in tune with values. It is the purpose of every judiciary to synergize justice and the law, yet reality demonstrates that they are often in conflict.

There are many examples of such conflict. During the apartheid years, for example, night sirens indicated that the streets had to be cleared of blacks. If black people remained in the open after that time, they were 'guilty' of breaking the pass law and arrested. This also affected whites in black areas. Whites had to have a permit to go into a black township and were not permitted to remain there after dark. If they did, they broke the law. There were laws such as the Immorality Act, which made it illegal to have sexual relations across the colour bar. The Group Areas Act prohibited people from choosing where they wanted to live, and made it illegal for blacks to own land in white areas (and vice versa). These are very clear examples of a huge gap between the law and justice.

So here we are – post apartheid and the new South Africa. All those laws have gone and justice is being done. Or is it? Is it right and just that the perpetrators of the atrocities and horrors of 'third force' activities are not charged and punished for their crimes? Is it right and just that the people responsible for atrocities and torture committed against dissident members of MK[†] in Quatro are not charged and punished for their crimes? What is just and fair?

Is it important to know whether or not they broke the law at that time? Surely it is justice that we pursue and nothing else? Perhaps the law allowed security force members to kill; perhaps the law allowed MK guards, at Quatro in Angola, to kill dissidents. But this does not make it right!

In our pursuit of justice we need to examine the entire fabric of society, our businesses, and the procedures laid down by law.

As previously mentioned, the basis of such laws was that of conflict. If one approaches business interactively, with all parties and stakeholders pursuing fairness, justice, respect, professionalism, productivity and wealth creation, the basis

---

[†] Umkhonto weSizwe – the military wing of the African National Congress during the time of struggle against apartheid.

of conflict is no longer appropriate. In fact, such laws can then retard progress. Surely, then, we need a new approach to the law, and one that is designed to enable the new paradigms of interdependence and co-operation. We need to 'narrow the grey' (see page 93) between justice and the law, and shift our legal paradigms to a new order. South Africa's legal profession is beginning to do exactly that, through its inclusion of 'lay judges' – ordinary people who, it is intended, will assist a judge in finding fairness in his rulings. The same needs to be done in all areas of business and community leadership. The community must agree that justice is being done.

Perhaps, in our pursuit of justice, we may have to break the law. But if our objectives are noble and in tune with the community's values, the law should take second place to justice. The law must change. Nelson Mandela, himself a lawyer, was kept a prisoner for 27 years for pursuing this very principle of justice.

Autocracy, strong leadership and participation

Strong leadership is not autocracy. Autocrats are generally dictatorial in their approach, often taking little or no cognizance of the opinions or wishes of others. They make things happen their way! The authority of an autocrat is usually unrestricted.

If you are an autocrat, you will endorse the above, and find nothing untoward about it, especially if you are successful at what you do. You will, through your experience, track record and history, justify why your autocratic approach has worked. But has it really? Have all the people you have led been wonderfully happy? Have they looked forward to coming to work every day? Have they willingly found ways to contribute more than is expected of them? If you are an autocrat, you will probably be thinking that none of these questions or their answers matter. As long as things get done efficiently and profitably, nothing else matters. Bear with me for a moment. Because of your autocracy, there are sure to be 'camps' in your business: groups positioning against one another and running to their own agendas. Some will curry favour with the autocrat, whereas others will be using every means possible – the law, the union, etc. – to limit or control the autocrat. There will be negative conflict, and such conflict leads to down-time, strikes, go-slows, inefficiency, and a general lack of productivity and profitability. There will be an increase in the amount of time spent managing crises and difficult or sensitive human resource issues. This is time that a manager could be using far more profitably if there was no conflict to resolve. From a business point of view, conflict costs money and doesn't make sense.

Economics aside, what about human beings? People are not machines. They have feelings, hopes, fears; they experience joy and heartbreak. This is Africa and it is emotional. How can there be happiness if one ignores humanity, *ubuntu*, and the collective? Surely it is the responsibility of leaders to enhance the quality of life of the people that follow them. Let's explore an example of autocracy:

Autocrats will not be keen to draw on the analogy between themselves and such a heinous individual as Hitler. However, Hitler was a dictator and an autocrat. To the German people he was presented as a saviour, someone to look up to and to follow out of the terrible depression of the 1930s. People wanted to follow him – he was charismatic, charming and convincing. But that was his public image. Behind the scenes he was ruthless. He cared nothing for the German people or their wishes. He only fed them with what they wanted for as long as it satisfied his personal needs and objectives. He created the Gestapo to eradicate any resistance to his ideology. (I know of many business and other leaders who display similar behaviour.)

At a senior level Hitler behaved very differently. He was utterly and openly dictatorial. There was genuine conflict among his senior leaders (his board of directors), to the point where some of his general staff attempted to kill him in 1944.

As an autocrat, charismatic as he was, he used song, charm and rousing speeches to instil unbelievable pride in the German people. Because he made them feel good about themselves and gave them hope, they loved him. But all of this was designed to foster loyalty to him alone so that he could better achieve his ambitions. Hitler lied to the people all the time. When ambition is coupled with dishonesty, one finds the evil of autocracy.

Hitler did not share his real goals with the people. He did not stand on a podium and talk of murder and genocide. Instead, he talked of love and care for the ordinary German people. This is the kind of thing that makes autocracy so dangerous. The autocrat is unassailable and need not even share his visions. People are therefore never empowered, and rely entirely on the autocrat. 'Power corrupts and absolute power corrupts absolutely.' Because of this, the wise leader in a position of power will devolve power to his subordinates. He will ensure that they have the power to veto any of his decisions. He will be totally reliant on consensus, notwithstanding his ability to persuasively influence the group. He will create mechanisms to ensure that he is unable to become an autocrat. An autocrat will never allow such a thing and, because of this, he will gradually be corrupted by the power.

Strong leaders

A leader is simply someone whom people follow. An autocrat does not always command the respect of those he leads, whereas a good leader does. A strong leader is able to make unpopular decisions and, because of the trust and faith people have in him, these will be respected and accepted. It usually becomes clear that even unpopular decisions are made for the right reasons and to gain the best results. As a result, even more trust is built in his leadership. None of this can be achieved without the leader becoming vulnerable and exposed. Leadership is vulnerability. By sharing a dream or a vision, by exposing hopes and emotions – or weaknesses – one can be hurt. One can be challenged and face failure. But if a person can do all of this and still have a following, it is seen as confronting a just cause. Do all the people who follow you know you well as a human being and trust you and your leadership? Do they know of and buy into your vision? Is that vision shared? Are people willing to accept your failures or will they desert you when things go wrong? Let's look an example of a strong leader:

Almost single-handedly Mohandas Gandhi confronted the mighty British Empire. He had a vision of an independent India – one that the Indian people shared. His own values would not accept violence as a solution, so, in consultation with the Indian people, the word *satyagraha* was created. Often referred to as 'passive resistance', it translates as 'the non-violent force which is born of truth and love'. Although the Indian people shared this view, they wavered and began to turn to rioting and violence after the terrible massacres by British colonial security forces. It was Gandhi who maintained the then unpopular stance against violence, in opposition to the people. Through his hunger strikes, he was able to get the people to realize that he would not waver and would continue fasting until he died, unless they stopped the killings. They stopped. His esteem, the aura around him, increased even further because of this. (This is what we have referred to as *seriti* or *isithunzi*.) The people wanted to follow Gandhi. His motives and integrity were open and easy to see. There was no hidden agenda. Although he did not seek power, he became powerful and influential. He was able to pursue his own dream, because it was shared by the people.

But Gandhi made himself vulnerable. He was incorruptible because he would not allow himself to even consider his own 'power', which was derived directly from the people. He held no official government office or position. His rank was recognized through his own good deeds – it was not something that was conferred on him or taken by him. It was won by him. Gandhi was not only a popular leader, he was also a strong leader who did what he knew to be right and moral, even if it did not always coincide with the wishes of the people. In doing this, he recognized that he could lose his following.

Participation

Participation empowers people but, more importantly, it leads towards democracy – and democracy takes power away from autocrats. Understandably then, autocrats have an aversion to participation. But if the leader is afraid to share dreams, if the leader is afraid to ask people to follow him, rather than tell them to follow, it can only be that he is afraid that, given the chance to decide on their own, given participation, they would choose not to follow him.

If the vision is just and good, if the values are shared, and one leads according to these values constantly, and if one cares deeply and sincerely about the people, the people will want to follow one. By involving the people in some way, one adds to personal esteem and gains more authority for the direction and decisions that are being taken. Using authoritarian terminology, one gains more power by constantly giving that power away.

Participation has a range of meanings in business. For many, it simply means giving the people the opportunity to share, by contributing their thoughts and ideas, while the final decision-making remains in the hands of the leader. For others, participation may mean taking part in the process, decisions, profits and leadership. Participation covers a wide field and 'participative management' has meant many different things – from advising the autocratic leader on the one hand to almost full democracy on the other.

The importance of the team

A good team is one that shares the vision of its purpose. It is motivated, passionate, caring, loyal and fit for its mission. Its members have total trust in one another and are comfortable discussing their individual weaknesses so that the team is protected from them. This implies honesty and a recognition that the individual, though always giving of his best, must be sublimated for the good of the whole. Let me share a personal story of vulnerability, of sharing weakness or, indeed, the failure to do so:

When I was 20 years old, I was a second lieutenant serving with 1 Parachute Battalion. I was unfortunate to have had a fairly serious accident while free-fall parachuting. Getting rid of the partially deployed main chute was no problem, but releasing the partially deployed reserve was! I hit the ground, fractured ribs, broke a leg and badly dislocated my left shoulder. But the most important injury at that stage remained invisible. I had severely traumatized my cervical spine and, within a few years, had to have a very large tumour removed to prevent paralysis and to reduce the pain. After these operations, I was left looking quite normal, but I had lost my ability to parachute jump or to strike the ground with impact, for this could result in a neck fracture. I was condemned to helicopter-borne operations only. Although my leaders knew, I was too proud to tell my own men about my new weakness.

In the late 1970s, I was on a military operation in Zambia when our convoy came under enemy fire. In leaping from the back of the troop carrier, along with the troops, I struck the ground hard and awkwardly. Something happened in my neck and I crumpled to the ground, paralyzed. I had to lie quite still while vehicles surged off the road around me and men ran firing into the bush. Through the smoke and haze, I could hear someone shouting to me, 'Are you hit? Are you OK?' I found that I was able to talk but I couldn't move. I called back that I did not think I had been hit, but that my neck could be broken. As you can imagine, the response from the bush was extremely uncomplimentary!

However, with considerable danger to his own life, one of the troopers crawled into the road, grabbed me by my webbing and dragged me into cover. Within minutes, my body began to feel pins and needles and, slowly, I began to regain normal sensation and movement in my limbs.

The issue is this: Because I had not accepted my own weakness, I was unable or, rather, unwilling to share it with my troops. They, in turn, had been directly affected by my lack of openness and inability to share. Had they known about it, perhaps they could have compensated for it in some way, and helped me to overcome it. I had not only risked my own life by being too proud, but I was directly responsible for placing another man's life in extreme danger. I know I can say, boldly, that all my men wanted to serve under me. They all told me this. There was great respect and trust among us, so why the fear of vulnerability?

This experience was a very important lesson for me. From then on, whenever I operate in a new team with people who do not know me, I describe my weaknesses in detail so that they know what to do if I encounter trouble.

Good teams mostly express their unity in a physical or demonstrative way. In many instances, this expression is through dance or song. Singing gives the team an opportunity to share in the expression of a single vision, emotion or belief, both verbally and passionately. The following words, sung by Umkhonto weSizwe soldiers, is an example: *Akekh' uMandela, usentilongweni, saze sawel' iKomand' ingenatyala* (Mandela is not here, he is in prison, we have lost a commander). An excellent example of a chant and dance is the haka performed by New Zealand's national rugby team. It is a very clear and somewhat aggressive statement of the cohesiveness of the team. Interestingly, it is of Maori tribal origin.

Most teams have symbols. Members are proud of the team, its members, and their own role in that team. Team leaders usually understand and nurture this.

There are many examples of excellent teams. Some of the best are military: the British SAS, the United States Green Berets, the South African Reconnaissance Commandos. Then there are national sports teams. Each of these teams have several things in common. Interestingly, apart from possessing all of the features mentioned above, each one comprises volunteers who really want to be in the team and have been selected. More importantly, they all share the same values. If they didn't, the cohesion of the team would be lost. So they are selected according to their values as well as their skills. The extensive psychological screening that every special forces soldier undergoes as part of the selection process is effectively a value assessment.

Autocrats very seldom create excellent teams. People usually work very hard and do what they should out of fear of such leaders. In teams led by autocrats there will be a corresponding lack of trust because of that fear. People can be fired or severely disciplined by the autocrat with very little recourse. There can be no openness, no honesty and no sharing of weaknesses for fear of dismissal or retribution. There can be no trust, because each member of this team runs according to his own agenda in the effort to protect himself at all costs. To achieve this involves currying favour with the powerful and occasionally treading on colleagues.

Autocracy, by its very definition, involves coercion. People will not do things because they care or are passionate about achievement, but because they are forced. They will be rushing to get to work, not because they love it, but because they need the money or are fearful. Team spirit will very seldom be evident in such groups. There certainly will not be spontaneous singing, or the sharing of pride in the organization. Singing may occur, but this will most probably be in rebellion against the autocratic leader.

Teams are often created out of conflict. Should there be a common oppressor, people who would not normally associate tend to create alliances. There are many examples of stress-produced team alliances.

Let's look at two simple examples of team allegiance on a hierarchy of loyalty. The one on the left is a team/community created by the place in which we work. The one on the right is created by what we are as human beings.

Workplace teams		**Teams of humanity**
The company		The company
National sales		All humankind
Regional sales	**Pressure**	Continent
Self and secretary	**forces**	Country
Self	**loyalty**	Race
	down	Tribe
		Clan
		Extended family
		Immediate family
		Self

The more extreme the pressure on the group, the lower down the hierarchy one's loyalty will settle. Likewise, as pressure is eased, one can afford to develop loyalty to the next group up on the hierarchy, while retaining simultaneous loyalty with the groups lower down the hierarchy. This type of hierarchy can be reproduced for the many teams to which we all belong simultaneously.

In Zimbabwe during *Chimerenga* (the fight for freedom), the largely Ndebele Zipra forces under Joshua Nkomo fought as allies with Zanu PF under Robert Mugabe. Immediately after the war, the two turned on each another as the unifying common enemy had disappeared. The same is true of the 'freedom forces' in South Africa. Nearly all were singularly united against the apartheid government. As soon as the common enemy was no more, the various movements positioned for power against one another.

The principle here is one of conflict due to self-interest. The 'team', which was strongly united, suddenly falls apart because its vision disappears. The vision of our African team must, therefore, not be based on enemies, but on what and who we are and what we can become. We should be united in a common cause, fighting common enemies, but those enemies should be things like poverty, unproductiveness, crime, anarchy and autocracy. The defeat of these enemies should be part of a process aimed at achieving a more noble and ever-evolving vision for ourselves and for Africa. To be truly powerful one must have a team. Great teams are self-motivated, democratic and share the same values.

Once again, Japan, Malaysia and Singapore are perfect examples. In Japan, one will even see visible reflections of value and team enactment. For example, the Matsushita Electric Company makes brands such as National, Panasonic, Quasar and Technics. It is ranked among the 50 largest corporations in the world.

...Every morning at 8 a.m., all across Japan there are 87 000 people reciting the code of values and singing together. It's like we are all a community.
    – RT Pascale and AG Iathos, *The Art of Japanese Management*

Another example is the widespread performance of t'ai chi – relaxation exercises that are designed to grow one as an individual – in Japan. This is endorsed by the entire Japanese community and is practically a cultural expression. So, although one is strengthening and developing the self, one is, at the same time, developing the community.

It is only by being strong as an individual that one can hope to be part of a great team. It is interesting to note that the Japanese symbol for humanity is '/\'. The '/' represents people, and the '\' the person. The one will not be able to stand without the other; there is total interdependence. In African terms, *ubuntu* is nothing unless there is *seriti/isithunzi*. Perhaps the finest achievement of true team is when one also becomes a community. A wonderfully complete description of this is found in the Zulu word for community – *umphakati* – which means 'We are all together on the inside.'

Democracy, mob rule and consensus

Democracy implies majority rule, fairness, respect, tolerance and a classlessness that recognizes the basic equality before the law of all people. It presupposes discipline, order and sophistication. In terms of decision-making, it is normal for a simple majority to carry motions, but a group may decide to change this for particular reasons in its constitution or group. The overriding feature of democracy is its orderliness and its thrust for fairness. The majority clearly leads, although minorities are always carefully considered.

A mob is a group of people that have decided they want something, but it is the antithesis of democracy. There is no order and minorities are quickly eradicated by the mob – in many instances through actual killings or other equally appalling acts of brutality. There is no tolerance for anything other than the mob's direction and energy, and anything in its path will be obliterated.

Democracy is not mob rule, for where democracy seeks to understand minorities and tolerates differences, the mob attacks them. Where majority decisions are taken by both, the democratic forum conducts itself with dignity, care and compassion; the mob by coercion, destructive energy and threat. Democracy seeks to give; the mob seeks to take.

Without adequate focus on principles and positive values, democracy can easily be hijacked and become a mob. The mob then continues to call itself democratic as 'the majority has decided' on a course of action. But when the values of the group no longer underpin dignified, positive, democratic norms and aspirations, it is no longer a democracy; it is an unruly, negative and destructive mob. Russia, under Stalin, is an excellent example of such an abrogation and hijacking – a complete shift from socialism to dictatorship and autocracy – and the ultimate result of mob rule. It is probably the mob factor that makes most business leaders so afraid of democracy.

At the opposite extreme of the mob is the concept of consensus, which suggests a collectiveness and inclusiveness in decision-making. It goes beyond simple democracy; a majority is no longer acceptable. In fact, it is very difficult to attempt to give consensus specific rules. It is something that is felt and there is usually a clear indication that consensus has been reached. Generally, those opposed to the direction become very aware that they are now part of the minority and quietly accept the broad consensus decision.

Consensus decision-making is only possible where there is trust and where a value system has become so meaningful that all the people believe in its intrinsic inviolability. People know that the group is trying to do what is right, and not attempting to promote a particular, selfish viewpoint. This is not as impossible as it sounds.

Because it is reliant on the feelings of the group, the intellectual side of the democratic process, important as it is, becomes only one feature of the group. And because of this reliance on feeling, morality and emotion, it is completely in tune with Africa. The process is comfortable because Africa is moral and emotional. I do not mean to imply that there is no intellectual argument and debate, but rather that there is an inclusiveness of all influences.

Consensus is an extremely advanced and sophisticated system that goes beyond simple majority rule and looks for a broader inclusiveness. It carefully listens to and considers everyone's views, and always bears in mind that the group is trying to do that which is right. It tends to overcome the polarisation of opinion that can occur within a purely democratic system – the thought that, if the majority thinks something is right, everyone else must be wrong. It demands a very high level of accountability from every individual. What needs to be pointed out, however, is the fact that it does not come easily and requires a great deal of hard work.

Let's take a look at a somewhat unusual example. During a particularly interesting time in Shaka's rise to power, just after his foster-father, Mbiya, had died, he returned to his royal home at Bulawayo and a chaotic state of affairs. Several incidents occurred that had all the people in a state of utter alarm for, according to tradition, these things implied witchcraft. Shaka ordered a 'smelling out' of the culprit by the famous sangoma, Nobela.

All the regiments were assembled and Nobela and her assistants began their terrifying task: running up and down among the ranks of warriors and maidens, jumping high in the air and screaming terrifying curses, wild-eyed and desperate, howling harridan-like and hissing at the frightened people to chant the traditional *siyavuma* (we agree). The low chant began to pulsate after each of her babbling outbursts, getting louder and then sometimes being so quiet that it sounded like a collective murmur. Each time Nobela made her way past someone whom the community did not like or who was under suspicion, the chanting of *siyavuma* would get very loud. As she moved away, the chanting would quieten down. In this way, she was able to make popular decisions.

This example highlights how close consensus and mob rule can become. Was this an example of mob rule or consensus? There was order and discipline in the process, evident by the control Nobela (and Shaka) held over the proceedings, but it was also the group's critical mass that determined decisions.

One might say that the majority determined the course of the decision, but this is an abrogation of consensus. Neither the group nor Nobela (nor Shaka) took cognizance of the condemned person's defence or situation. They were not even heard. In other words, the minority did not have a voice at all. It is probably this that we all fear.

How do we go beyond the extremes – autocracy and mob rule and the fear of both – towards inclusiveness, synergy, democracy and consensus? By letting go of all the negatives. By letting go of what we are and of all our current fears. By letting go in favour of what we can become.

PART 3

CHAPTER 8

▲▲▲▲

What we can become

The massive task of transforming a nation like South Africa and a continent as crippled as Africa into a world power seems, at times, quite impossible. But it is not impossible. All it takes is for us to get on and do it.

Perhaps the most powerful example of the vision and fortitude that we need can be given by a person far more qualified to do so than I. Early in 1995, I had the great privilege to meet and talk with Li Lu, the Chinese student leader of the protests that culminated in the 1989 massacre in Tiananmen Square, Beijing. He spoke of his hopes and dreams for China – of the freedom and democracy he wishes for the Chinese people. He knows that to achieve this will be a long, lonely and difficult battle, but to illustrate the fortitude of the Chinese people, he related this old folk tale:

There once was an old man who was coerced by the powerful to live with his humble family on the slopes of a high mountain. Theirs was a difficult life of poverty and struggle, yet they were constantly working to improve on what little they had. One of the most difficult things for the old man and his family was the location of the stream from which they were forced, by circumstance, to draw their water. It was on the other side of the mountain.

One day, a neighbour was passing the old man's home and he saw him moving piles of stones off the mountain and into the valley below. The next day he saw the same thing, and the next, and now the old man's entire family were helping with the labour.

'What is it that you are doing?' he asked the old man.

The old man replied, 'I am unable to live on the other side of the mountain for reasons beyond my control, and yet that is where we draw the water we need to live. Being unable to move my home I have decided to move the mountain. I know that this task will not be completed in my lifetime, or even in the life of my children or their children. But one day, future generations of my family will be able to drink of the cool waters of a mountain stream that is easy for them to reach.'

Africa needs people like this: people who will not accept that things cannot be changed; young women and men who understand that although they may not reap the fruits of their labour, future generations will. Africa needs people who believe that the joy of contributing positively to a process that improves life for all, is life itself.

Interactive leadership

The following pages will, at the very least, unsettle any traditional views of leadership. In Africa, *umuntu ngumuntu ngabantu* (a person is only a person because of other people) and leadership exist in this context of humanity. In discussing leadership, I do not refer to dictators or autocrats. For them, humanity in itself is totally unimportant, except insofar as it can be used to gain their own selfish ends. Then again, they do not display leadership as leadership is something that people follow willingly.

We have all read and learnt many things about leadership. We have learnt to mentor, to coach, to be good role models; we have studied and, from our own experiences, have designed new motivational systems. If we didn't already instinctively know this, we have even learnt about the importance of caring for the people we lead. All of the literature and all of the paradigms assume a simple hierarchy: someone leads, others follow. Herein lies the essence of change. It is assumed that some people are leaders, and that others are not – the old nature-nurture debate!

I do not wish to draw a line between the two, for each has its place and they interact with each other. For some, leadership is easy. These people are born knowing instinctively that they have a following and they lead automatically. Others need to be shown where to begin. Through nurturing, many people realize that they do have innate and sometimes very powerful leadership capabilities. Nature then plays its role. True leadership and growth occurs through the interaction of nature and nurture.

To make fire, the ancient firemaker would hold a softwood stick under one knee and, using both hands, rapidly twirl a hardwood stick in a depression set in the softwood. The drilling motion would cause friction and the dust created would begin to smoulder and glow. With quick but gentle blowing, and the careful addition of dry tinder, one could create fire.

Leadership is like this. Some people are born knowing how to start the process, how to make the fire. They know instinctively that they don't have to fear it. Others have to be shown. Some people struggle when it comes to adding the tinder, but they learn. Once the fire has caught, the original firemaker is relatively unimportant compared to the designated guardian of the fire.

It is the guardian of the fire who gradually realizes that he 'leads' the fire. He can make it burn high or low, gently or with great heat, through the things that he does to it. The guardian who thought that he knew nothing about fire, not being born with the knowledge of firemaking, is now an accomplished expert in the use of fire.

The first leadership challenge for all human beings is to lead themselves. This is probably the most difficult task of many people's lives. They have to make decisions, move in a particular direction, and determine strategies to achieve objectives. More frightening is the fact that they need to be accountable and responsible – at least to themselves. As soon as a person is willing to accept that accountability, he has become a leader. Acceptance of accountability takes great courage and this is the foundation of leadership.

Courage is something that people respect and, because they respect it, they listen to and are guided by the behaviour of courageous people. The guidance of a respected colleague is often easier to accept than that of senior leaders or managers which may be regarded as suspect. This is especially true if a person has *seriti/isithunzi* which has been enhanced through courage and actions that their colleagues respect. This lateral reliance on colleagues for guidance and leadership is particularly evident where there is not an open and trusting relationship between the ranks or hierarchy of a group.

In the film *Hook*, in which Robin Williams played Peter Pan, there is a very good illustration of what I refer to as interactive leadership. Granny Wendy is the central character of the scene. She is a wonderful, gracious, kind and sensitive woman, and has been responsible for the care of hundreds of homeless children. She has seen to their adoption and integration into the world, and has loved them and given them all a sense of belonging. She is a pivot around which they can develop their lives. A hospital dedicates an entire wing to this amazing lady and Robin Williams, who is chairman of the board, and an orphan who owes his life's successes to Granny Wendy, is asked to talk at the function.

He delivers a deeply moving and personal speech about Granny Wendy. The people are riveted and very moved by his words. They share his love of Granny Wendy and, stimulated by his words, while he is still talking, a man rises and gently, softly, blows a kiss to the wonderful old woman. Almost immediately, another person rises and bows to her. Robin Williams continues to talk. Another person rises, and then another and another – each sharing his or her own appreciation and love for Granny Wendy. Robin Williams continues to talk. Sensitively and emotionally, he uses words to describe what everyone is demonstrating.

Who is the leader? Robin Williams because he has an audience that willingly follows him? The first man to rise, breaking protocol, in the middle of the speech to blow a kiss of honour to Granny Wendy? The second, third or fourth person to rise? Who is the leader? Are they all leaders? At what point do the people demonstrate leadership or following?

A leader whom people willingly follow (in this case, Robin Williams), facilitates the interaction. The first man to rise is also a very powerful leader, for it is from his example that others in the group (the audience) take their cue. Respecting his courage and honesty, members of the audience are encouraged to share their inner feelings, to become vulnerable and exposed, to stand and physically demonstrate their respect and love.

This is interactive leadership. They all become exposed, vulnerable and accountable. Through this accountability, they become leaders and others follow them. They do not ask to be followed – others simply do. But without Robin Williams, they would not have exposed themselves. He, too, is a leader – a coach. As soon as they accept their accountability, they become leaders and they become empowered. They understand that they can choose when to follow him and when to take their own course. A good, strong leader encourages this.

Interactive leadership is the interaction and resultant growth and progression that occurs when individuals demand and encourage accountability, first of themselves and then of each other. It is accepted that all people are or can become leaders, even if the only person they lead is themselves.

It is my belief that we can all be leaders, and that there is a progression of leadership. Let us look at some interesting examples that reflect this philosophy.

When one thinks of the military, one would be forgiven for thinking 'autocratic' and 'no questions asked'. But within this massive international military system (and every nation has one) there are amazing and perfect examples of democracy and interactive leadership. In many special forces worldwide, the structure is based on a group of four men who operate together. This number was deliberately chosen to avoid the emergence of a leader in the classic sense. Without ever having defined it as such, special forces treat every individual as a very capable leader.

Each person exercises his own individual perception and judgement at full stretch.
                                                    – T GERAGHTY, *Who Dares Wins*

Perhaps Colonel David Stirling, founder of the British SAS, best summed up the capability of each person to become a leader when he said:

We believe, as did the ancient Greeks who originated the word 'aristocracy', that every man with the right attitude and talents, regardless of birth and riches, has a capacity in his own lifetime of reaching that status in its true sense…
                                                    – T GERAGHTY, *Who Dares Wins*

To be aristocratic is to belong to the very highest level of society. Yet David Stirling says everyone is capable of achieving this. However, he does put in the rider 'with the right attitudes and talents'. Here is the challenge of interactive leadership: to nurture but also to attack; to encourage but purposefully unsettle in order to grow those attitudes and talents. In our terms, they amount to one thing only: accountability.

Society is not a reflection of a carefully selected military unit. Yet the principles of democracy or consensus and respect for individual capabilities and potential should be no different. There are many amazing and moving stories of ordinary people who have risen to the need for leadership, and who have become accountable under the most trying and tragic circumstances. We have all heard of quiet, little old ladies who have taken charge at road accidents, floods or earthquakes. What is it that stirs in these situations? Stories abound of ordinary people who do amazing things in times of emergency.

During World War I, on 21 February 1917, the troop ship *Mendi* was transporting a section of the South African native labour contingent from England to France, when it was involved in a collision with another vessel. The night was particularly dark, with visibility further obscured by thick fog. The *Mendi* began to sink immediately. In the chaos caused by the darkness and the sloping deck, it rapidly became clear that there would not be time to clear all the lifeboats from the deck. This meant that many men would not have a place on the lifeboats that had been launched. The water was freezing and many of those who jumped into it died from extreme cold.

As the ship began to slide under the waves, a lone voice called loudly to those who knew, without doubt, that they were about to die. It was the voice of the Reverend Dyobha, who had been recruited as a clerk and interpreter.

'Be quiet and calm, my countrymen, for what is taking place is exactly what you came to do. You are going to die... but that is what you came to do... Brothers, we are drilling the death drill. I, a Xhosa, say you are my brothers. Swazis, Pondos, Basutos, we die like brothers. We are the sons of Africa. Raise your war cries, brothers, for though they made us leave our assegais in the kraal, our voices are left in our bodies.'

And they took off their boots and stamped the death dance on the deck of the sinking ship.

— NORMAN CLOTHIER, *Black Valour*

This heart-rending courage, dignity and acceptance of life's final challenge – to die with dignity – exposed those amazing men for what they were. There is nothing in the world that could have forced them to do something they did not want. Led by a great man, who was not their appointed leader, and based on their individual courage, they faced the inevitable fear and became accountable to themselves and to each other and prepared to die with dignity. They chose to dance, and they led and supported one another to achieve that final dignity.

I weep at the tragedy, but I also weep with pride. For in dying in this way, they showed us how futile we are when we refuse to accept what we are capable of.

Values and principles

The first step in building an interactive leadership system commences with values. Most people, when asked to list values or principles that describe their life, have considerable difficulty differentiating between the two words. Both words appear colloquially to be used to describe 'good' and 'meaningful' things.

However, there are clear differences between the two words and we need to understand them, at least academically. Stephen Covey, in his powerful book, *The Seven Habits of Highly Effective People*, defines values as 'the way things should be'. In other words, they are things we strive for, although our environment, country or business may not necessarily reflect them at that time. Values can and mostly do change over time.

For example, prior to the 1960s, Western society was generally conservative when it came to the issue of premarital sex. Even discussing the subject was frowned on. Then along came the hippie era, with Janis Joplin, Joan Baez, Bob Dylan, The Beatles and The Rolling Stones, flower power and 'Make Love – Not War' posters. There was a complete rejection of traditional and conventional values, and promiscuity proclaimed in the 'free love' of the hippie movement became accepted by an entire generation of youth. The Western world shifted its values, even if not quite to the extreme of the hippie movement.

Another example of shifting values emanates from what is now First World, democratic England, where freedom of speech, movement and the equality and dignity of all people are not questioned. Yet, between 1680 and 1700, British vessels transported some 300 000 slaves from Africa. Still later, '…after the Asiento Treaty [1713] had opened up South America, traffic in human beings became a virtual British monopoly' according to WL Langer in *Western Civilization*.

There are similar examples of value changes in African society. Different tribes throughout Africa maintain the need for large families. Children are regarded as a blessing from God, and the ability to have children is a test of manhood and a source of social pride. In addition, children care for their elders in old age, and it is therefore good security to have many children. Population growth and birth control issues are alien. Yet these values are shifting gradually towards smaller families with the increase in education.

Principles are fundamental world truths and do not change with time. The same things appear in every major philosophy and religion in the world. They are universal truths that reflect our humanity.

Even so, many people confuse values and principles. In certain African languages there is only one word used to describe both concepts. When asking tribal and Third World people about values and principles, it is preferable to ask: By what rules do you govern your own life? For this reason, values in this book must be seen broadly to include principles and even behaviours.

The creation of values, and attempts to connect them to productivity and performance, is not a new concept. But what one does with values and how they are incorporated after they have been created is the point where significant divergence occurs.

Many management teams create values and then thrust them on the organization. I heard this comment from a senior leader of a well-known international corporation: 'We [the management] listed the values and then went to each factory and office, and spent a lot of time explaining them to each group. Nothing really changed though and, quite frankly, other than the teambuilding senior management experienced during the time in the bush, when we listed the values, I think it was a bit of a wasted effort.'

This demonstrates that values cannot be simply created by one group and imposed on another. It is not just the values themselves that are central.

It is the attitude to values that is important. Values do not exist alone and separately. They form part of individual belief systems and are therefore integral to every decision and step that each person makes. They are what we represent as human beings. To be accepted by a community, values have to be created and shared by that community. By accepting them, the individual is accepting a way of life.

Once values have been honestly and sincerely shared, democracy automatically follows. It is only on the basis of trust that sharing can occur. This positions us, as a community, for a completely alternate and African way of interacting. But before we investigate this matter further, let's look at value creation itself.

Value creation

There are two ways to create values. The one is democratic and the other is to decide on them autocratically and then actively sell or impose them on a community. The latter is referred to as imposed values.

A good, if unfortunate and tragic example of imposed values can be found in Germany under Hitler's rule. When Hitler rose to power in the 1930s, he had a clear vision of what he wanted: a powerful, unified military Germany that controlled Europe. With this in mind, he purposefully set out to militarize the minds of the German people – to create military values. First he fanned their sense of indignation with the humiliation of defeat in World War I. By doing this, he was effectively getting the nation to examine itself and to decide what it did not want to be. He was roadmapping. The people did not want a 'defeated' Germany. Then he gradually introduced values such as pride, using patriotism as the key, and recreating the old lie: *Dulce et decorum est pro patria mori* – the willingness and the passion to die for the fatherland. He created, among other things, the Hitler Youth League, ensuring in this way that he was able to mould the young leaders of Germany around his values, which were designed to put Germany on a military footing.

Hitler created what became a popular radio programme, called Strength Through Joy, which combined entertainment, holiday discussion and education, but all of it was filtered with Nazi indoctrination. To demonstrate his 'care' for the German working people, he created the Volkswagen Beetle (or people's car), to provide cheap transportation. He romanticized the Aryan people by promoting German music, art and culture with one thing in mind: the myth of the super-race. He needed tools to sell this concept to the people, so he hosted the Olympic Games in Berlin in 1938 and was directly involved in the creation of Aryan heroes.

In 1935, he made an absolute mockery of the Versailles Treaty (the treaty that ended World War I and demilitarized Germany) by marching unopposed into the Rhineland. This escalated the perception of German invincibility and further added to his cause. These and many other such steps gave Hitler immense pres-tige among the German people, and he was able to use this to further fan and cre-ate pride in the military values he was so keen to instil. Hitler gradually imposed the values he wished to achieve on the German people.

There have been other equally insidious examples. For hundreds of years, the world has seen the creation of the myth of white superiority over black races. But is it a myth if whites and blacks have come to believe it to be true? Blacks and whites have been conveniently stereotyped into groups akin to master and servant. In many instances, both groups believe these things about themselves to the point where the values coupled with this attitude are almost unassailable. The values are so firmly entrenched, and the culture is so solid, that the greatest battle is to get people to realize that it is they who imprison themselves in this bigotry. No amount of finger-pointing at the opposite group will release them. Only they can do that for themselves.

Growing up in a small rural community, I was exposed to many examples of social programming. At the time, not too many people – especially youngsters – even realized what was happening. During apartheid times, a siren used to sound at 10 p.m. For white children, all this meant was that it was bedtime, but it was a signal that all blacks had to be off the streets as the towns were completely 'white by night'. This often criminalized ordinary, law-abiding black people who simply worked late and then had difficulty getting home. If they were seen on the streets after this time, they were arrested for infringing the hated pass laws and would often be locked up in jail for a period as punishment for this 'crime'.

Every child is taught to respect the law. These people broke the law and were therefore 'bad' in a child's mind. To see bands of 'criminals' being marched along the road – all of them black – subtly reaffirmed that black people were bad. After all, one never saw whites in groups of convicts. 'White is all right' became quite understandable and the concomitant values of confidence, leadership and baasskap[†] over blacks followed automatically. It took quite a lot of mature thought to realize that an insidious system was at work. Even if this realization did occur, conditioning would be so deeply ingrained that breaking free of

---

[†] Loosely translated, this means master-servant superiority.

apartheid itself could leave one with the behavioural prejudices derived from formative conditioning.

A white friend related the following story about himself, which illustrates how deeply the conditioning process and dehumanizing of blacks affected people:

One day, with the grey-headed black gardener working close by, the little white boy was finishing off a lunchtime sandwich and playing with a friend. With the half-eaten sandwich now unwanted in his hands, he turned, shouted 'Here!' and flung it, laughing, to the gardener. It hit the ground in front of the man. The black gardener slowly stood up and, looking directly at the little white boy, said, 'I am not a dog.'

My friend was ten years old at the time. His family was not racist, but the entire white society acted in a way that was simply reflected by children. They became conditioned by life views that completely disregarded the humanity of blacks.

Don't be misled and believe that we are pointing only at the evils of apartheid in South Africa, for it has not been confined to South Africa alone.

In the United States during the 1960s, there was widespread civil disturbance over these very issues. The enrolment of James Meredith as the first black at the all-white University of Mississippi sparked off a massive riot. In 1965, there were race riots all over the South and these spread rapidly to other cities. Prominent black leaders, such as Martin Luther King and Malcolm X, were assassinated simply because they pursued equal rights. There were, of course, significant gains made by moderate, accommodating people, both black and white, but the cost in lives and bitterness was high. The echoes of these hard racial attitudes and prejudices are still heard in the United States today.

When I was 18 years old, I was an exchange student in the United States. After trying to explain, with some difficulty, South Africa's separate development policy to a large group that I was addressing, a gentleman in a stetson and boots drawled out this line which was met with much mirth from the audience. 'Well son, I guess what we should do is ship all of our blacks out to y'all in Africa in exchange for all South African whites and I just know we'll solve one hell of a lot of problems!'

Implication? Blacks are no good. Whites are good. Welcome to America. Whites are all right!

All over the world one sees racial prejudice, the result of imposed values, at work. This is obviously unacceptable. We are people with different cultural backgrounds, languages, histories and colours, but there is no super-race. There is no race of losers. There are simply good and capable individuals, irrespective of their racial or cultural heritage. We need to break free from our own conditioning, and only we can do this for ourselves.

CHAPTER 9

The path to democracy and sharing

Imagine you are lying on your death bed. Gathered around are your family and your close friends. As you look around, you see the people whom you love and cherish most in life. Everything fades for a moment. The voices seem to echo. But there is one voice you can hear quite clearly. It has been asking questions persistently. It is your own voice.

'Have you lived your life well? Have you lived life joyfully and given love freely? Have you come to the end of your life knowing what it is to be truly human?'

What would your answers be? Do you give love – or is that too 'soft' a question to be asking a disciplined and controlled pragmatist? Do you really know the real joy of interacting with people who are close to you, and the joy of knowing they care for you?

Often, we hide behind a veneer of professionalism and intellect. We build great screens that shut out real contact with people. We are mostly wary of exposing ourselves to others, fearing the pain and anguish that deep and complete vulnerability can bring. So we don't allow it, and prefer to bluff and bluster our way through life as 'the real success story', 'the real professional everyone looks up to'. But do they really, or is it just a flirtation with the materialism we represent? After all, if one has managed to accumulate wealth, it is regarded as something to be proud of. Is this all there is to life?

A short while ago, I had a discussion with a business associate. He is immensely successful and involved in a range of businesses. He owns properties around the world, a yacht in the Mediterranean, a villa in Portugal, and another in France. Yet he is lonely. His life has no meaning. More than anything in the world, he wants to meet a special partner who will make him feel happy and fulfilled. He wants to be married and have children, and have the time to develop deep and close friendships. But all his searching is outside of himself. He has not examined himself to find the root cause of his unhappiness. He has lost touch with humanity. He uses all the right phrases, talks about care and family and emotion, but somehow it is all empty.

There is a way for him to experience real life, but this involves exposing himself, becoming vulnerable and cracking the veneer of being an efficient machine. He needs to share his loneliness with, among others, the people he leads and works.

Every manager and leader will be thinking to himself that this is in no way similar to his own situation. After all, he is not lonely – he is surrounded by lots of people who respect him. Dig deeper. How do your staff feel? How many of them can you honestly say would come to you with their deepest feelings? Perhaps this will tell you whether you are lonely or not.

In a Group Africa survey in which directors and senior managers were asked whether or not they, as leaders, were lonely, 70 per cent said they were. However, it is necessary to distinguish between the loneliness of leadership decisions and loneliness caused by purposeful isolation from colleagues or community. Why are people lonely when they are surrounded by capable professionals? There is only one reason. It is because they have lost the ability to share. They no longer know how to, because vulnerability has come to mean weakness. They pursue and laud what M Scott Peck calls 'rugged individuality'.

Sharing involves community, trust, respect, honesty and loyalty, and it presupposes these values are in place.

Most leaders are lonely because they do not share anything, including leadership. For various reasons, they believe that, as the leader, they will make the best decisions. This may be true for purely professional issues, but not for issues related to values. No person is capable of routinely responding to value challenges the way a group will respond. For this reason, if the leader persists in taking value-related decisions alone, he will gradually alienate himself from the group – not because the group believes him to be bad, but because they see him as separate from and not representative of themselves.

It is fascinating to analyse and correct problems with values or, rather, as I prefer to put it, value infringement.

For all of these reasons, it is important to be in a team with other people who share the same values. As a result, decisions are easier to make and trust is built. Everyone works and lives to the same agenda. One can be human and share the concerns and pressures of life and leadership. But more importantly, one can give those who follow, the joy of discovering intrinsic capabilities and leadership potential.

Without imposing values, how can one go about creating them and become part of a noble and caring community?

Interactive forums – the *umhlangano*

Before any system can be put into place, there has to be a structure through which it can be implemented. Discussion groups or 'interactive forums' must be formed

(Group Africa calls these *umhlanganos*†), gathering and grouping departments or sections that work together. These groups involve everyone in the department, including managers and union officials. No one is exempt and nothing has greater priority. During these discussions, rank does not exist. All the participants are simply human beings baring their humanity and listening to each other with dignity.

We should bear in mind that a suit and tie was at one time regarded as authority, and authority meant trouble for the people. Try to find ways of breaking down this conditioning and the perception it conveys. Perhaps dressing more informally – especially on *umhlangano* days – and then raising this as a discussion point could help. Once people have attended a few *umhlanganos* and understand the process, the chairperson need not be the normal departmental leader. He can be appointed by the people. However, chairing such a session is not easy and, until the process is well entrenched, a suitably qualified individual (not necessarily the department head) should remain in place.

The subjects for discussion in the initial sessions are things on which no one person has licence. Every human being has a right to have his say about values. This is a forum in which opinions can be aired. The *umhlangano* can also make decisions. These must be by secret ballot, and achieved through consensus. However, the forum can only make decisions about things for which it is responsible and accountable. As the upholding of values is something for which everyone is responsible and accountable, the forum can make decisions that affect values. Similarly, the rules of consensus should be determined by the *umhlangano*.

The *umhlangano* should meet for around two hours, once every four to six weeks (and more frequently in the beginning). Through these forums, the entire basis of *ubuntu* will be reflected in your business for the first time. Remember: *umuntu ngumuntu ngabantu* (a person is only a person because of other people). It must be emphasized that there is no rank at this forum – just a group of human beings. Gradually, people can be encouraged to raise any issue they like.

For example, a matter in which the strategic direction of the company is questioned could be raised. Questioning is fine and should be encouraged, and the chief executive officer (CEO) must ensure answers are forthcoming – even if it is to say the matter is confidential and to explain why this is the case. The forum cannot make decisions regarding company strategy as it is neither responsible nor accountable for strategic issues. However, if the strategic path conflicts with values, the forum has a right to be directly involved and even to decide against accepting the strategy. Such a session would need to include the management personnel who are accountable for the strategy.

An example outside of the African environment is the United States and its policy of involvement in Vietnam. The decision taken by the United States gov-

---

† *Umhlangano* (Nguni) = discussion/interaction

ernment (the national CEO and his management) to get involved, conflicted with the values of the American people, who then had a right to halt the strategy. Protest and mass action forced the United States government to listen to the people (the *umhlangano*), and to withdraw from Vietnam.

It is important to make a few cultural and historical observations about an *umhlangano*. This system is based on the traditional concepts of *amandla* (ordinary strength or power) and *ibandla* (the strength that comes from many people). Traditionally, it was the *ibandla* that guided the king. It gave him the opportunity to read the consensus of his people.

The opposite of an *umhlangano* is an *umbango*†. In an *umhlangano*, maximum positive criticism and creative energy is generated. In the *umbango*, one finds individuals who negatively criticize to achieve their own ends – perhaps even to dethrone the leader. In an *umhlangano*, criticism is made to strengthen the leader and one another. There is a very fine line between the two concepts. South Africans, in particular, because of recent history, tend to have difficulty differentiating between the two. In the *umbango*, one argues for position. In the *umhlangano*, one argues to build and strengthen what is being created.

One of the ways in which the *umbango* gains strength is to nullify positive arguments, refuse to participate and to intimidate anyone whose thrust is towards openness and togetherness. This is achieved by creating subversive dissension and fear, by isolating the leaders of the positive thrust and attempting to discredit them. An effort is made to position the leaders as the enemies of the people.

In the past, one would often hear the word *impimpi*‡. Roughly translated, this means 'sellout'. It was and sometimes still is used to stop people from participating openly with one another, and, more particularly, with management. In this way, one shifts from an *umhlangano* to an *umbango*. Forcing the openness of all procedures and discussions works directly against the *umbango*. Openness works against politicking and the formation of camps. In an open environment, the *umbango* will die.

Democratic value creation

If you believe in democracy – the true spirit of democracy – then you will have no problem with democratic value creation. But most business is not democratic and therein lies conflict. Democracy in business? Many people will say: Sure, as long as it's controlled!

---

† This means a vendetta, or a family or tribal feud. It can even mean an instrument used to achieve witchcraft. However one defines it, there is no doubt the gathering is negative, subversive and destructive.

‡ The word *impimpi* originated in the early settler days, when white landowners ran large black labour forces. They often wanted to know what was going on among the ranks, and they would pay a particular individual, perhaps in brandy, to inform them. They would call this person their 'pimp'. A spy who was controlled by some form of blackmail became known as an *impimpi*. The term is, therefore, very derogatory and fear-laden. In later years, suspected *impimpis* were often necklaced or killed in equally barbarous ways.

It is ironic that people who decry autocracy in government, and go to extreme lengths to ensure government is democratic and open, are, given half a chance, absolute autocrats when it comes to business.

If one believes there are certain universal truths, principles that are core to all humanity, you will have no difficulty pursuing democratic value creation. It involves a process of questioning, discussion and voting on values. The questioning is not as simple as it sounds. Without trust, people will be suspicious of the motive behind the question and will not necessarily speak out. Patience and integrity must prevail and, as people learn to trust the leader, they will open up and begin to participate.

But how does one go about democratically creating values? The first question to the *umhlangano* is simple: What values are really important to you as an individual? By what rules do you govern your life?

Encourage people to simply call out words. No discussion should occur at this stage. Write down every word or phrase that is called out. From time to time, throw in your own words to ensure you are a participant, part of the group, and keep urging the people for more. Once they appear to have exhausted their own list, get them to look over it and check whether there are other values they would like to add. Don't rush. Bear in mind they are likely to have given you values, principles and behaviours. Don't intellectualize – just write them down.

Starting with the first value on the list, institute a discussion on what it means to the group (see 'Narrowing the grey' on page 93). At the end of the discussion, everyone will have a clear understanding of what the particular value means to the group. Now vote (secretly) on whether the value should be accepted or not. You will have to discuss exactly what constitutes the motion being carried – perhaps 90 per cent of those present, or even more – before you vote. Use consensus rather than a simple majority for this crucial step in deciding on values. Once consensus is fully understood by everyone, you will not even need to vote, but this will take time and trust. Consensus is a reflection of the general leaning towards decisions and will meet with little resistance. The decision should feel right to everyone present – even those who disagree. If it doesn't, people will complain loudly.

If the value is accepted, write it up on a separate overhead or flipchart for everyone to see. Now do the same for the next value. Start the discussion and end it with another vote. Take your time and don't rush the discussion. Repeat this until every original word raised by the group has been covered. This process may take several sessions but, at the end of it, you will have a list of values the group believes are really important to them as individuals. You, of course, are part of that group and shared in the process.

An example of the types of values that may be important to people is indicated on the following page:

English	Sotho	Xhosa
Care	*Tsotello kapa khathallo*	*Ukukhathala*
Understanding/ good interaction	*Kutlwisisano*	*Ukuva/ukulandlela*
Respect	*Hlompho*	*Ukuhlonipha*
Pride in what we do	*Ho ikhantsha ka seo re se etsang*	*Ukuzingca*
Openness	*Ho Buleha*	*Ukuthetha phandle*
Listen and hear	*Ho utlwella le ho utlwa*	*Thembeka*
Loyalty	*Botshepehi*	*Ukunceda*
Pro-active	*Ho etsa*	*Mamela/yiva*
Natural drive	*Thahasello ya ho atamela*	*Ukufunda amanye* to
Draw closer to other cultures	*haufi meetlo emeng*	*amasiko*
We are 'Of Africa'	*Re ba Afrika*	*Singa ma-Afrika*
Trust	*Tshepa*	*Ukuthemba*
Honesty	*Botshepehi*	*Ukunyaniseka*
No 'them and us'	*Re khannwa ke mphato eseng ('bona' le 'rona')*	*Sibanye*

Now that the group has created values, you need to ensure the company combines its values lists. You must end up with only one list that is accepted by the entire company or community.

There is no reason for the company not to be in absolute agreement with the values listed. After all, the leadership participated in the creation process and had ample opportunity to argue for or against particular values. The process has, in fact, reduced conflict and brought various players closer together. It has done away with 'them and us' and created a 'we'. If the value is on the list, it is because the majority of people believe it should be. And that's consensus democracy!

Through this shared value creation exercise, everyone – including management, union and staff – has effectively agreed to buy into and uphold the values. Make sure this is stated categorically and that everyone agrees. Before we continue, we need to cover value negotiation or 'narrowing the grey'.

Narrowing the grey

When discussing values, I make use of a very simple model. From a leadership perspective, there are three areas one needs to be aware of when dealing with values:

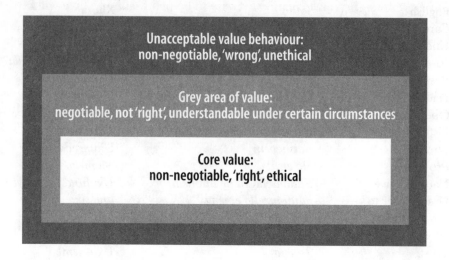

The objective of leadership is to narrow the grey area or, if you prefer, to reduce dissonance. A cohesive team experiences minor dissonance in the shared values of the team. They experience different attitudes, but not different values.

That which is 'right'
The centre of the model – the core – is the area of value assessment which the individual regards as 'right'. There is a complete and unbending understanding of the value at stake, and any behaviour contravening this will be considered unethical. For example, a tenet of the value 'honesty' is that one never steals. If you are among colleagues and you see a R100 note lying under someone's chair, you don't keep it, you hold it up and ask who has lost some money. This behaviour is considered 'right' and displays the individual's understanding of the value 'honesty'.

That which is negotiable
Surrounding the core is a grey 'negotiable' area. Here, the value is constantly tested against a subliminal hierarchy of personal values. For example: Although it was not right for the man to steal, he was stealing food for his starving children. In this instance the value of 'care' for the children has greater weight than the value of 'honesty'. It doesn't make the theft honest, but it does make it understandable.

That which is 'wrong'
The third and final band is that which the individual simply considers 'wrong'. This is the flip side of the core value area. An example of unacceptable or 'wrong' behaviour may be: The man has a good job and lives well. However, he took the lady's handbag and stole all her money. For the individual concerned, this is wrong, dishonest and not negotiable.

Do not expect the value creation exercise to be plain sailing. There will be disagreement and this should be encouraged. At first, people in the team may try to avoid exposing themselves through discussion. But when they realize the process will continue regardless, they will, at the very least, participate in deciding whether or not to adopt a value. Indeed, if a secret ballot is used, the chairperson, with witnesses, must count the votes in full view of everyone. If he or she comes across a spoilt ballot, the counting must be stopped immediately and the whole voting process repeated. In other words, everyone in the *umhlangano* must vote either for or against an issue. This forces accountability. No one can be a spectator or a passenger in such a critical exercise.

The process is as important as the outcome. The group as a whole is narrowing the grey or gaining a clear understanding of what each value means to the group. The group determines each value's boundaries and defines acceptable and unacceptable behaviour regarding this value. Maximum discussion and participation is therefore crucial.

You may notice that people will attempt to gauge what the popular leaders think before committing themselves. It is important to keep pointing out that this is *ubuntu* at work. If an individual – be it the CEO or the most charismatic leader in the group – is followed blindly, the individuals in the community are not deciding for, and therefore leading, themselves. They are subtly avoiding their own accountability. Don't allow the process to be hijacked. If it is, all that happens is that centralized leadership shifts from you to another individual, and not to the group and each individual in it. The people will, in many instances, consciously or unconsciously be trying to shift centralized leadership to another individual. Resist this by persuasively pointing out what is happening. I often mention to groups that we are in the process of empowering the group, and pursuing something the group wants. An individual or a few representatives cannot be allowed to take on that power. They are not the group and the individuals must accept their accountability and responsibility.

There will probably be several sessions in which values will need to be discussed. Later discussions should be a lot easier than the first session and people should be focused only on the values and what they mean. The process of narrowing the grey, in particular, should test each individual's core beliefs and paradigms. They will have exposed themselves as individuals and become vulnerable, but you will start to notice a drawing together of the entire group. This gradual formation of a new, complete team, a new community with shared values created by all and agreed to by consensus has, in fact, simultaneously been creating trust.

Once this first step of creating the interactive forum or *umhlanganos* has occurred, and values have been democratically created and shared, it's time to move on to the next step in the building process of African interactive leadership.

Interactive leadership

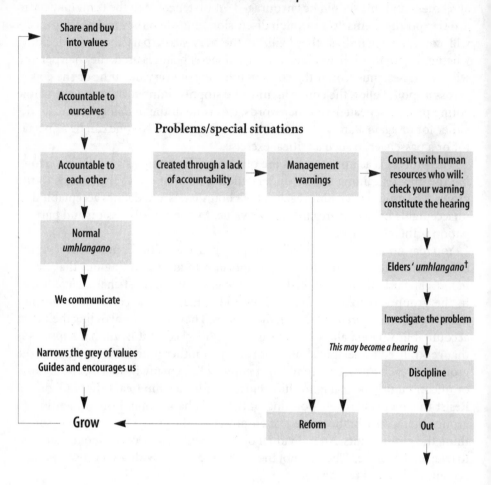

Problems/special situations

▲▲▲▲

CHAPTER 10

Accountability to self

Being accountable means fully accepting responsibility for our actions and decisions. This is very easy to talk about, but in practice it is a completely different matter. Most people squirm in their seats when they are pinned down to a specific action for which they are accountable. Most will try to find flaws in the instruction or look for loopholes that will allow them to escape accountability should things go wrong. People seem to do this instinctively. Rather than pursuing ways to succeed, the instinct is to escape by avoiding accountability.

This is equally true of values. Once the value creation exercise has been completed, everyone in the group becomes accountable for upholding the values and must say they will do so. Yet, some of the first debates in narrowing the grey will demonstrate the need for people to leave escape hatches open. They will try to avoid too narrow a definition. Even more interesting is the fact that the group will accept values for the group, but will look at them very differently when told that these need to reflect their personal views, for which they will be held accountable.

The first active step in interactive leadership is to become accountable to ourselves. Only by doing this can we hope to interact with others with integrity and honesty. How can we talk about and debate, for example, the values 'professionalism' and 'honesty' in an *umhlangano* if we are neither professional nor honest? How can we discuss trust and care, when we neither trust nor care for the individuals in the group? The starting point, therefore, has to be to challenge ourselves and our colleagues to self-examination. As trust grows, people begin to realize the debates and discussions help to narrow the grey in their own views of these values. It is no longer just an intellectual exercise, but a deeply personal one in which we begin to feel exposed and vulnerable. Through that vulnerability, as we expose our weaknesses and our emotions, we come to understand ourselves better and, because of the constant intellectual and emotional challenge, we grow as individuals. We are forced to think about values we previously perceived only from our own viewpoint. Now we are challenged by different paradigms; we are forced to decide and become accountable to ourselves. This is a wonderful and exciting interactive step. We empower ourselves and are encouraged and pushed to grow even more by our colleagues.

Progression of leadership

Phrases they use

Concern for others

Visionary leadership
Impassioned and
charismatic. They share
their dreams.

*I have a dream I know you
share. This is the dream…
I care for you.
I know that if we proceed in
this direction, things will be
wonderful*

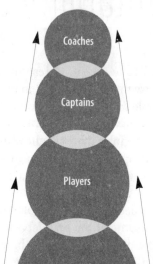

Coaches

Physical leadership
Positive and motivating.

Captains

*Let's try this. I'm sure it will
make a difference. See, like
this…*

Enquiring leadership
Generally positive even
if the team is not win-
ning at the time. They
know their efforts will
enable the team to win.

Players

*Shouldn't we be trying some-
thing different? I'm sure it
will work better if we do.*

Observer and critic
Only positive when the
team is winning.

Spectators

*This is a disaster! They should
wake up and do something
about it.*

Concern for self

It is for the leader to encourage the leaders within us all

The progression of leadership

There is a degree of leadership in every person. All people can be encouraged to
develop and demonstrate 'dormant' leadership qualities. All leaders, at all levels
of progression, are responsible for nurturing, stimulating and awakening the
leader that exists within practically every human being. This is the nature of leadership.

Successful organizations are surrounded by very vocal leaders – leaders who
question, who insist on finding better ways, and who demand higher standards
of those who lead them and those whom they lead. Traditionally, leadership has

been firmly viewed as the realm of the line manager and the shop steward. The Progression-of-leadership model alternatively views all people in the organisation as potential leaders.

Leaders generally have an excellent understanding of the levels below them *vis-à-vis* their view of more senior and more junior leadership. However, people understandably, and generally, do not have a good comprehension of issues higher up the leadership progression. It is the responsibility of the more senior leader to constantly share his world with those around him, so that they may grow.

I believe that all people progress through different phases as they grow as leaders. Some people start high on the progression, whereas others never make it to the top.

The Progression-of-leadership model divides people into four broad groups: spectators, players, captains and coaches. Spectators make up the greatest sector of humanity. These people are observers and critics, and they are only positive when the side is winning. They have a high concern for self and are very critical of change agents. Although negatively critical, they will very seldom do anything to change the circumstances they dislike. They simply prefer to get more vocal and more negative in their criticism of 'appalling leadership' when things do not work out to their satisfaction. Circumstances rarely work out to the satisfaction of spectators, so their primary characteristics are negativity and selfishness. I'm sure everyone has heard someone say: 'They should do something about it. This is a disaster.'

Spectators never expose themselves and avoid the concomitant vulnerability at all costs. It is as if they instinctively know that by becoming vulnerable, they will be challenged and forced to become accountable for their own actions, views, utterances and behaviour. Spectators are characterized as negative, selfish and highly critical; they never expose themselves, refuse to accept accountability and are often devious.

Spectators are not leaders. Indeed, they represent the greatest challenge to the rest of the group as they not only inhibit but, in many instances, actively work against the progression of leadership in others. These are the people who will very quickly but deviously position someone as an *impimpi*. It is they who will make it known that an individual, who may be doing well and, in so doing, drawing close to the manager, is 'flirting with the powerful' or 'sucking up to the boss'. This can occur even though the individual may be making an amazing contribution to the progression of the organization. Their intention is to create a 'them and us' syndrome, to divide the team. This is *uMona* at work.

Are you a spectator? Can you think of people around you who are? By their very nature, bureaucracies breed spectators. I must point out that this model in no way implies that spectators are junior staff and that coaches are the most senior players. It is quite possible that very senior managers are spectators, and some of the most junior people in the organization, captains and coaches.

Orthodox leadership would view these spectators as 'the enemy'. They may be problematic, but they can be viewed differently. The Batswana say, *'Oseka tlhoya motho tlhoya molata'* which means, 'Do not hate the person, you must hate the matter'. The challenge of leadership is to grow people away from spectatorship, to stimulate maturity and to nurture the leader inside them.

Fortunately, all people can progress vertically up the model. But they will do so only if there is interactive leadership at work. Every member of the group needs to help to grow every other member. A single, strong, centralized leader – charismatic, inspiring and good as he may be – will not manage to actively encourage the personal growth of all the individuals he leads. People may love him and want to follow him, but the likely response is for them to become more reliant on the central leader, thereby avoiding personal accountability and growth. Growth is dependent on the group or the community, but it will not happen unless people are accountable to each other.

You will notice that between the clear groupings on the model there is an overlap of the two influences. So, for example, in the first step up the progression, one is both a player and a spectator. This implies that an individual's behaviour will fluctuate between the two: sometimes acting like a spectator and other times like a player. This is a very difficult and stressful period for the developing leader, who is realizing and understanding true personal accountability for the first time.

Players are the next stage in the progression and represent the start of real active leadership. These people are generally positive, even if the team is not winning. They understand and recognize that their own efforts contribute significantly to the team's winning potential, and they accept this accountability. Not yet experienced or confident in leadership, they begin enquiring about possible alternatives. They realize that by asking, they are doing something positive and contributing; they are making a difference. Spectators will see this and, although negative, distrustful and cynical, they will respect the courage of the player. They will, however, attempt to persuade the new player that exposing their vulnerability is dangerous and foolish. Simply asking whether or not there is a different way, positively, with real intent to find a solution through the enquiry, the player becomes vulnerable. Players' leaders should react positively and encourage this behaviour as it will encourage confidence and progression.

Alternatively, players' leaders could be insensitive to the courage it has taken for the spectator/player to make this transition. By ignoring or dismissing a tentative enquiry, they set the new player back. Players will immediately go into 'I told you so' mode and regroup with the spectator.

However, once the player has established a basis of trust and confidence in the position, leaders will take more cognizance of the questioning. Through this recognition, the player is encouraged to become a player/captain. The individual's *seriti/isithunzi* is enhanced. Captains display physical, compelling characteristics. They are positive, motivating and confident in their acceptance of themselves.

They have a high degree of concern for others and are extremely sensitive to the difficulties experienced by people lower down the hierarchy. They are not afraid to become vulnerable and they do so through the acceptance of accountability for their own actions. They do not necessarily volunteer deep personal feelings. However, if they are asked to share them, they will do so, initially somewhat hesitantly and curtly, but as they grow, more fluidly and easily.

Once again, vivid examples can be drawn from the traumatic circumstances people confront in war. The following example of a 'captain' is once again from the sinking of the *Mendi* in 1917:

As the ship sank lower in the water there were still blacks aboard who were too afraid to take to the water. Some of the white NCOs continued to urge them to jump. Prominent among these men risking their own lives and even using physical force to get the men to jump, was an Afrikaans-speaking sergeant-major. There were two sergeant-majors on the Mendi, *of whom one survived. Richardson is said to have jumped overboard to encourage the blacks to follow him and to have come aboard again. He was last seen … still helping men to get out of the forward hold. It is probable that he went down with the ship.*

– NORMAN CLOTHIER, *Black Valour*

Coaches are the visionaries. They are impassioned, charismatic, and they share their dreams. In doing this, they completely expose themselves emotionally and are often ridiculed. However, because they are charismatic, people will follow them, sometimes unquestioningly!

Coaches are not always captains, and at times are not very good physical leaders. They often have the ability to envision but not to implement. They have an extremely high level of concern for others and this adds significantly to their charisma.

In 1963, Martin Luther King epitomized the image of a coach when he stood in front of the Lincoln Memorial in Washington DC and gave his famous, 'I have a dream…' speech to 200 000 people.

President Nelson Mandela shared his great charisma and vision with the world at his inauguration in 1994. It drew an entire nation – indeed the world – into his dream for the future:

We shall build a society in which all South Africans, both black and white, will be able to walk tall, without any fear in their hearts, assured of their inalienable right to human dignity – a rainbow nation at peace with itself and the world.

The coaches/captains are the most mature and well-balanced individuals. Both charismatic and physically motivating, capable of sharing dreams and making them happen, these people are highly respected by the group.

The lowest denominator or behaviour one displays sets the level at which one is perceived. For example, if you are a captain 99 per cent of the time, but slip, negatively criticize and observe without doing anything to promote change, you are, in fact, a spectator. Your position becomes one of spectator, and you lose the captain's spot.

Carefully assess your position apropos the Progression-of-leadership model. Now, take the model and give it to two or three colleagues and, without telling them your own thoughts, ask them to plot your position. You need to emphasize that it is the lowest denominator that positions your attitude and approach to life. Is there a difference between your own and your colleagues' views? If there is, discuss it with them. Don't try to convince them that yours is the correct assessment. Listen to what they have to say and thank them for their contribution. The more people you ask to do this, the better the picture you will glean of yourself, and the more you will be able to grow.

A significant dichotomy between your colleagues' views and your own view can indicate several possibilities:

1. You don't expose yourself to the group, so they simply don't know you.
2. You don't listen to people in your group sensitively and with intent to hear.
3. You don't trust one another and so the dichotomy displays hesitancy or cautiousness.
4. You don't know yourself very well.

A solution to this rather serious problem is to have more frequent, more vulnerable discussions in the *umhlanganos*. This should have been happening in the *umhlanganos* already, particularly through ongoing discussions about values. Remember, it was your personal view of the value that you were supposed to share. Discuss yourself personally and then listen and hear others. Don't get defensive. Leadership implies an acceptance of responsibility and an accountability for one's actions and position.

Leadership

There are some interesting perversions of leadership that are directly related to an inability to accept accountability. The first is what I call an 'irresponsible charismatic'. Some people are simply charismatic and, because of this, others follow them. But if the individual refuses to acknowledge he has a following to whom he is accountable, he becomes dangerous. He is able to move rapidly, even negatively and critically, against very positive and well-meaning leadership. Because he is charismatic and has a following, others may emulate him and a negative movement can be created. The irresponsible charismatic in isolation is no problem, but the effect of such a person on a group is unbelievably destructive. Until they accept their accountability to the people who follow and emulate them, irresponsible charismatics are exceptionally dangerous, even evil. Beware of them. However, with careful guidance, an irresponsible charismatic who is not bad, just irresponsible, can become a true and amazing leader. In many instances, this person will fit into the captain/coach area and be of tremendous benefit, not only to the group but to life. Don't waste them, however difficult they are to lead.

Irresponsible charismatics must not be confused with mavericks. Mavericks are unorthodox and independent-minded, but this does not make them irresponsible. They acknowledge their own intellect, capabilities and responsibility, at least to themselves. If they are charismatic, they will have a following, but it is their acknowledgement of that following that makes the difference. There is maturity in a maverick that is missing in an irresponsible charismatic, although a maverick will be just as difficult to lead. He will not be negative or destructive, but he is sure to be disruptive by constantly breaking from custom.

Leading and interacting with mavericks is one of the most rewarding, if challenging, leadership experiences. A maverick who buys into a process or system can become one of the most dedicated protagonists of the approach. After all, he personally challenged every aspect, investigated every alternative, and made every adjustment he felt was needed before he did!

A leader's power is derived from those whom he leads. The people whom one leads give that leadership power. The charisma and ability of the leader will encourage people to support and follow him, and their support will grow his power. As the power grows, so will his confidence and ability to demonstrate his capabilities. This in turn will lead to greater support, and so, greater power. However, power in isolation corrupts, and a wise leader will ensure that as powerful as he may be, he gives overt recognition to the fact that the people are the power and he is answerable to them. They should be able to censure him for contravening values. If there are no such mechanisms in place, he should help the people to create them – in other words, help the people being led to lead him.

The people should lead the leader, guiding him as he grows in his leadership role. As long as the leader is able to listen to, and hear those whom he leads, he remains free of arrogance. When he no longer hears his followers, he no longer leads – he forces. This is the difference between leadership and management. Management, by its very nature, implies control and coercion, whereas leadership implies offering an example others will follow willingly. Management implies command, whereas leadership is personal example, facilitation and persuasion, discussion and challenge. Leadership is the ability to encourage colleagues and followers to challenge – vigorously, persuasively and actively – and, after discussion, to accept the best course of action, which may not necessarily be the leader's own.

Leadership is doing what is right, even though it may be unpopular. It is knowing that decisions are right but unpopular, and that they build rather than take away respect. Leadership is understanding the fine line between strong leadership and dictatorship, between democracy and mob rule. It is accepting one's intrinsic leadership.

In every environment there has been a significant shift from management to leadership. The primary principle is that only people who are respected, knowledgeable, capable and enlightened will lead. Rank should not be something that is imposed – it should be earned. What the individual represents is important – not the position he holds. This principle is crucial in an African environment expressing *ubuntu*. If people are empowered and understand that they can openly question and challenge without retribution, they will very quickly point out when leadership is lacking and when it is good.

Mature leadership dictates that we routinely and constantly attempt to employ people who are more capable than us or who, at the very least, have the potential to be. If this does not happen, the organization will, over the years, gradually slip into mediocrity and disappear. The culture of employing less capable people is perpetuated by the people we employ, who in turn employ people who are less capable than them, and so on. To reverse this takes enormous confidence.

By employing people who are 'better' than us, we become driven. By surrounding oneself with ever-better people and by stimulating their personal growth, one empowers the organization, giving if life, passion and fortitude. They push us, challenge us, and force us to learn, grow and lead in ever-improving ways. Should we reach a level at which we can no longer progress, and those following us can, we must accept that it is right for them to overtake us. We do, after all, think highly of them and respect them, because that is why we brought them into the organization!

The individuals we have helped to grow are perfectly positioned to lead us through interactive leadership. It is not a negative situation, but pride is one of the most difficult issues for a leader to confront. Could you let a more junior leader leapfrog your position? Would you be willing to offer support? This is not something that comes naturally, but it is something that needs to be discussed and gradually accepted. The group will counsel the leader through such a process.

Normally, when the time arises, the leader will leave the environment to maintain a dignified withdrawal. But why should your skills and experience be lost to the community you are so much part of and have led? Because of pride alone? No. We should continue giving our maximum, possibly in a different role. We should be able to say with pride: 'It is because of us that these great things are being achieved. It is because of us that we have these amazing and special people who, in turn, are employing amazing and special people.' However, one should also be mature enough to leave if it is the right thing to do.

It is the paradigm through which we view withdrawal from a leadership role that makes the difference. If we are all leaders, if every one of us is aware of other people's strengths and weaknesses because of the open and honest way communication takes place in our *umhlanganos,* such a step is considerably eased. Everyone will already know about most of the issues, and individual capabilities and potential. What a wonderful, positive message of humility and capability you send to the team. You are encouraging the rest of the team to attain their individual capabilities and not to be limited – not even by yourself.

▲▲▲▲

CHAPTER 11

Accountability to each other

The first step in interactive leadership is to buy into a value chain. We then have to be accountable to ourselves for behaving according to those values. The next step is to accept our accountability to each other. In other words, we have a collective accountability. The following example of collective accountability, taken from a study of the Zulu custom, is practically universal when referring to the traditional African way.

The whole kraal is responsible for the misdeeds and debts of any one of its inmates, and a principal is always responsible for the acts of his agents or dependents... The result is that every man in the tribe is a policeman, and is bound to report to his supervisor any act or wrong which he may see being done, otherwise he incurs responsibility in regard to the act.

– EJ Krige, The Social System of the Zulus

Interactive leadership involves leading one another; leading and being led by colleagues regardless of their position in the organization. This also assumes equality of humanity, without discounting individual *seriti/isithunzi*, and a collective aspiration towards superordinate goals. What is your group's superordinate goal? Giving people an increased market share percentage or a beautifully-worded mission statement outlining how the group undertakes to be a good corporate citizen has minimal appeal. It is too distant, too unreal for most people.

These goals can be reduced to tangible features by creating a culture conducive to achieving goals. The culture is defined by values and that becomes the superordinate goal for the group. It is something everyone can understand. It is possible to relate honesty, care or professionalism to the individual, and it is quite possible to be more honest, professional, efficient and effective. However, the fact that this converts into a greater market share or reduced crime is not the focus of the individual. By maintaining a clear focus on values, no one will be confused.

Colleagues and an ever-improving, maturing and more open and honest group, are well aware of one another's personal successes and failures. By this, I do not mean the rep's big sale or the extra production that was churned out under great difficulty in the factory. The manager will be focused on these. Rather, it is the moments of personal triumph that no one, other than the person seated right next to you, sees. It is the time when you made that difficult telephone call and successfully put pressure on a client to pay. It is the time when you needed to be really honest in a business relationship and, despite fear of rejection and hurt, you summoned the courage to address it and did so well. It is the time when you stood alone against a group who were being unprofessional and told them so, even though you had no line authority. Your manager will probably be unaware of these things, but your colleagues will not. These are the individual's triumphs and failures. Is it personal? If it had to do with your workplace and your growth, it is not only personal, it is also a matter of concern for the group. They can encourage you, grow you. Indeed, this is what makes the difference in interactive leadership. The group is accountable to you to ensure you grow from successes and failures, and from everyday challenges. These positive successes should be raised in *umhlanganos* by the colleagues who see the acts.

Let's explore how accountability to each other works in practice. The first part of this is easy. Individuals are encouraged to talk to each other. This is not gossiping. On the contrary, whereas gossiping is used to destroy, normally because of self-interest or ignorance, and always because people have no forum to openly discuss behaviour, this is a building process. When you build and are accountable, you talk. Remember the difference between an *umhlangano* and an *umbango?*

For example, if I see someone infringing a shared value, I am accountable to raise this with the individual. If the behaviour does not change, I should raise it with someone who can do something about it, or in a forum with everyone present. This process of personal accountability works directly against the African concept of *uMona*. For want of a better description, this is the 'tallest poppy' syndrome. If you stick your head out or raise it above the group, it is seen as exposing the group and pressure will be brought to bear on the individual to retract. This can extend to threats of violence, witchcraft and even death, and needs to be taken very seriously.

The response is to alienate this approach by creating a new and more powerful community. Shared values and openness disallow *uMona*. Protagonists of *uMona*, who are always spectators with high self-interest, are regarded as outsiders. Delicate as it may be to raise, many new black managers, in South Africa in particular, are either unwilling or unable to discipline their staff. The reason is simple. During the freedom struggle, *uMona* was used as a control. Anyone standing against the group was in severe danger. This culture now disempowers many managers who were a part of the struggle.

However, there is a new community and the struggle is against polarization, disempowerment, low productivity and inefficiency. The new community must stand together against all negativity. It will only do so if its cause is just, has integrity, and if the people remain accountable to each other. Values give it a firm base. Leaders must be aware of the enormous courage it takes for any individual to stand against *uMona*. But people are very capable and, led interactively, they will do this for the thrust is towards goodness.

Routine *umhlangano* management

Umhlanganos are the vehicle through which everyone has an opportunity to share in the management and leadership of a company. The constant discussion around values relative to actual behaviour in the community narrows the grey, guides and encourages. You may wish to refer back to page 89 to remind yourself of the structure of an *umhlangano*.

Issues that are raised are mostly dealt with by the group, and each individual is empowered to, and does, make a difference. This leads to tremendous satisfaction and happiness, and builds a very powerful community and team. In environments where such communities exist, the joy of it is almost tangible. Unprompted, visitors will comment on the 'lovely atmosphere' or the 'easy and fluid efficiency of the team' or the 'spirit of togetherness'.

It is a wonderful way to work. But getting to this point isn't easy. Business traditionally engenders a culture which dictates that the manager's decisions carry the most weight. Interactive leadership can only operate in a community environment where such autocracy has been dismantled. This may require unlearning autocracy and re-learning democracy.

Part of that democratization is the recognition that everyone is treated in the same way, and according to the same principles and values. This equality is a direct reflection of *ubuntu*. Where such a foundation of trust has been laid, the *umhlangano* then guides its members. Practically, this is how one runs an *umhlangano*:

▲ Place everyone in a circle so there is no hierarchy.

▲ Move people around so there are no 'power blocks' seated together.

▲ Place a flipchart in a gap in the circle.

▲ Start the session by reminding everyone of the shared values by asking them to call some of them out. Stop on a particular value every now and then and ask people to describe what it means to them. This should take about 10 minutes.

▲ Now ask if anyone has anything they would like to talk about.

▲ Stand poised at the flipchart and, as people call out an issue, write it up on the board. In this way, you are creating an agenda. People will call out things like: parking, honesty, punctuality, toilets, socialization and work, and many others. Don't question or discuss any issue at this stage.

▲ When the list of topics has been exhausted, tell the participants they are free to add to the list during the discussions. In other words, there is no limit on what they can talk about.

▲ Starting with the first point on the board, ask the person who raised it to elaborate. Once this has happened, ask for discussion. Don't offer immediate solutions yourself and don't be afraid of silence. Encourage people to talk, and when they do, thank them. Do not judge them in any way. When discussion appears to be exhausted, offer what you believe you have heard as the solution. This must be based on what the people have said. If there are several possible solutions, approach it in the following way. Ask whether the interactive forum *(umhlangano)* is responsible and accountable for the issue. If the answer is 'No', let the group know you will raise it for them in the arena which is responsible and accountable. If the answer is 'Yes', vote for the best solution. Voting should only take place once the discussion has clearly elaborated the advantages and disadvantages of each solution.

▲ Once you have fully discussed and concluded the first issue, move on to the next one. Keep minutes of the decisions and read them at the next *umhlangano*. Be sure to note the person who is responsible for making the changes happen, and indicate a definite time frame for these to be achieved. This constantly reminds people of their accountability.

▲ Get through as many issues as possible in the time allocated to the *umhlangano*. The issues that are not covered must be raised at the next *umhlangano*. The list must roll from one session to the next. It is a living thing.

▲ If there are many issues outstanding and people keep adding more, you may have to call for additional *umhlanganos*. Clearly there are lots of problems that need to be solved, and people become frustrated if they are made to wait.

Even sensitive issues can be raised where the group will counsel an individual back on track if he wavers. For example, there may be someone who constantly infringes a value, or someone whose behaviour is upsetting another member of the group. Should such an issue be raised, it must be addressed immediately. Don't make the individual wait until everything else has been discussed. Escalate personal issues directly to the top of the list.

The *umhlangano* will address it using the process outlined below. Bear in mind this is not something that can be spread over two *umhlanganos*.

Summarized counselling process
1. We assume the person with the problem or concern has raised the issue with the 'offending' individual (we'll call this person Bloggs). If they have not, tell them to do so and ask them why they have not. If they respond or you believe it is due to fear of the individual, proceed to Point 5.

2. Nothing happens. There is no change in Bloggs's behaviour over the following days and weeks.
3. A routine *umhlangano* is held. The actual counselling process starts here.
4. The concern or issue can be raised in this way: 'I have a problem with Bloggs. I don't know if this is a personal problem affecting only me or one that affects the whole forum?'
5. The facilitator checks that the person with the problem has already raised it with Bloggs. If he has not, ask him why not. If he indicates it is due to fear of the individual, proceed as below. If there is no fear, ask the person to raise the matter privately after the *umhlangano*.
6. The facilitator explains the process to everyone as follows:
    'Bloggs, you will leave the room while the forum discusses whether it is affected or if it is a personal matter between you and the party raising the issue. If it is a general matter, we will discuss it before we call you back in.' Remind everyone of Points 8 to 12, so that there is no confusion regarding the procedure.
7. Ask Bloggs to leave the room. Offer reassurance.
8. Remind the forum of the values and get agreement that they are paramount.
9. The individual must state the specific problem.
10. The facilitator establishes whether or not this is a general (majority) problem by a show of hands, or by secret ballot if the matter is of a sensitive nature.
11. Discuss the problem and determine the values that are being breached.
12. Prepare for Bloggs's return. A spokesperson must be appointed to talk to Bloggs on the group's behalf.
13. Write the word 'Care' on the first page of the flipchart so that Bloggs understands that the whole process has been carried out with his well-being at heart – that is, the group cares for Bloggs. List each problem, the value that is being infringed, and suggested solutions on a separate page to enable Bloggs to address each problem separately. The spokesperson takes Bloggs through each problem.
14. On the last page, write the word 'Care' again, to emphasize how much the group values and cares for Bloggs.

This process can be used for the hierarchical leader. No one is exempt in their accountability to each other for the values. Let's have a look at an actual case. In this instance, it involved the leader!

Case 1
After 10 or 15 minutes of discussion, it was very clear that there was a block to normal communication. Something was clearly preventing discussion. As the facilitator, I asked the chairperson if I could speak. I then explained the counselling process and emphasized that it applied even if the leader was the problem.

Immediately, Sandile, the leader of the region, asked the *umhlangano* whether he was the problem that was creating the communication difficulty. Several people responded by saying that, although they were not sure he was, it was probably a good idea if he excluded himself. Before leaving the room, Sandile ensured another chairperson was appointed. Up to this point, my task had been to check that the correct order and protocol was maintained in the *umhlangano*.

While Sandile was out, the *umhlangano* discussed him as an individual *vis-à-vis* the problems some of them were experiencing. As each issue was raised, they determined whether or not it was relative to the *umhlangano* or to only one or two individuals. One issue was clearly relevant to only one person and this was to be handled personally. It was not discussed further. However, there were several issues raised that everyone felt affected the group.

The first was what they called Sandile's 'amnesia', and it was listed on the board as exactly that. What they meant was that he sometimes forgot about things they had raised with him – things that were important to them as individuals. For whatever reason, Sandile either did not respond because he didn't think they were important, or because he genuinely did forget about the issues. Frustration among the people was starting to create friction. They thought that by not following up on the things they raised, he was being disrespectful. He was not listening to and hearing them. These were the values they felt were being infringed.

The second issue was 'lack of assertiveness'. They pointed out that they really wanted Sandile, on occasion, to firmly discipline them, when they knew they were out of line. In their words: Everybody needs to be disciplined sometimes. Sandile appeared unable to do this. The group's interpretation was that he was so much part of the team, he was starting to forget the fact that he was also their leader. The values infringed were professionalism, effectiveness and discipline. After each problem had been identified and connected to a value infringement, solutions were discussed in detail.

Before Sandile was brought back into the room, a discussion was held on how they thought he was feeling. Everybody agreed he would be feeling fairly rotten, and that it was clearly not an easy process to go through. They then decided they would try to ease things by joking with him when he returned. The technique the group decided on was to place a chair in the middle of the *umhlangano* circle, to set things up to look like an inquisition. When Sandile came back in, they said very formally and very firmly, 'Come on, Sandile, sit here.' There was a pause as his face dropped, then everyone burst out laughing, patted him on the back and said: 'Don't worry, come and join us in the circle.' This relaxed everyone. The group then reassured Sandile that it was not an inquisition, but was intended to be a positive building process.

Joseph had been elected as the spokesperson. He was very nervous and said so, but, as he had accepted his democratic responsibility, he began raising the issues one at a time. He summarized Sandile's amnesia as the *umhlangano* had done and pointed out the value infringements. He also outlined the solution raised by the *umhlangano.* They did not believe he was intentionally or vindictively ignoring them, and their solution echoed this sentiment. They suggested he place greater reliance and trust in his support staff. His secretary could have more control over his diary and help to direct his life. This would ensure that issues were followed up. Sandile said he now realized that there was a problem, but he had been totally unaware of it. He tried to justify his actions, but was silenced by the chairperson. This was the time to listen to and hear what his colleagues were saying. He apologized profusely and accepted that their solution was a good one. In the presence of the *umhlangano* and according to their suggestion, he conveyed the responsibility directly to his secretary. He asked her to chase him for follow-up whenever necessary. However, it was pointed out that he remained accountable.

The lack of assertiveness which the *umhlangano* regarded as unprofessional and ineffective, was an issue Sandile accepted fairly easily. He recognized that he needed to be firmer with his staff from time to time. They pointed out that he was not assertive enough, not because he was not a good leader, but because he perhaps felt so much part of the team. He appeared to be side-stepping the fact that he was their leader. They suggested he approach the training department and get himself onto an assertiveness course.

Once all the issues had been discussed, Joseph asked Sandile how he felt, and counselled him back into the team. Sandile was clearly relieved at the way the process had worked out, but mentioned that it had been very difficult for him. Even so, he felt relieved, elated and encouraged by the way things had been managed, and by what he had learnt about himself and his colleagues.

The last point the *umhlangano* raised was that they really cared for him and wanted him to remain their leader. There was a lot of emotion at this point and it showed.

There were some very interesting developments immediately after the meeting. The first was that several people asked the *umhlangano* if it would be possible for them to go through the same process – in other words, to be sent out of the room during a future *umhlangano* and be appraised at length. Several people thought this would be an excellent way for them to develop and grow as individuals as it had been such a positive process for Sandile. This is interesting as the perception of such a process is normally that it could be damning and negative. However, when it actually occurs, it is an extremely positive, counselling-type occurrence. The big difference is that the group is counselling a person and discussing values, regardless of rank. This is, in fact, a standard interactive leadership process called a 'mutual appraisal'.

Mutual appraisal

Based on trust, the mutual appraisal is the most dynamic and positive tool with which to grow each individual in the team. The process is also a powerful force in developing trust and care among team members. In a mutual appraisal it is the individual's colleagues who conduct the appraisal. Specific times are set aside for mutual appraisals. They do not form part of a normal *umhlangano*. The individual being appraisal must have our full, undivided attention.

Summarised mutual appraisal process
1. The facilitator prepares the team by raising the values. A short discussion on two or three values occurs. The forum is told that this is a mutual appraisal.
2. The candidate is asked to leave the room.
3. List the individual's strengths and weaknesses. Check that there is consensus on each one.
4. The spokesperson must rehearse the presentation in front of the group. No examples must be given. Raise only the issue under discussion. For example, 'The group find your very abrupt approach unsettling and unnecessary. Please take a little more time and address us all politely. We all like you but become irritated when you address us in that way'.
5. The candidate is brought back into the room. The 'care' that the group has taken over this process is emphasized.
6. Work through each strength and weakness and issue raised.
7. End the session by reassuring the candidate that the group really cares and hopes that this process will grow the individual.

The first step in creating values is complete. People are accountable to themselves and to each other, and the *umhlanganos* are enjoyable, non-threatening gatherings. Now the process of firmly shifting leadership into a new paradigm must be pursued. Already, classic managers have begun to realize they have the same voice as everyone else. They can no longer rely on threats and coercion. They understand that *seriti/isithunzi* gives them power.

Beyond the *umhlangano*, people may still try and resist the democratization process. Many managers do this, especially those who are very weak leaders. Many strong, popular leaders who are not managers, do this in an attempt to hijack the power they see being shifted away from the central leaders. If this occurs, these people will be discussed and counselled at the next *umhlangano*. If it is very bad, an emergency *umhlangano* can be called specifically to address a hijack issue and the individual leading it.

The challenge is for everyone to act, work and lead according to their shared values. Nobody can be exempt. This should not need to be forced as everyone normally sees the advantages of such an empowering and democratic path. But there will be other problems to deal with.

PART 4

CHAPTER 12

Dealing with problems

In the military, there is a classic principle: an obstacle not covered by fire is not an obstacle. In other words, unless you shoot at someone while they are crossing coils of barbed wire, they will find a way across. In our analogy, the values are the 'obstacles' between acceptable and unacceptable behaviour that must be guarded. Problems are created through a lack of accountability to values. Because the entire community shares in the creation of values, it is the community that must deal with the problem – as is the traditional African way.

Problem 1: Representation

The ultimate goal is to have the entire *umhlangano* together each time a problem arises. However, this can sometimes be impractical as a business cannot shut down at short notice to resolve value conflicts. Once the system is running routinely and people are truly accountable, very few value conflicts tend to be experienced. Although there are always regular *umhlanganos,* they are often scheduled too far into the future to deal with an active and potentially harmful problem that needs immediate attention. What happens if this problem arises? The leader is no longer empowered to act alone. It is important to emphasize that the best solution is for the affected community to go into *umhlangano*. If this is absolutely impossible, elders can be used.

Elders

One solution is to ask the people whether, under emergency circumstances, they are willing to allow representatives to act on their behalf. I have never experienced a case (where trust has already been well established), where people are not happy with this arrangement. However, this should only occur once the entire community has become accountable and has managed itself for a period of time. Without this prerequisite, people can use the elders to avoid accountability.

The first step is to elect elders: good, wise people whom colleagues believe represent and uphold the values that have been created by the group.

It is very important to point out to the group, including the elders, that this does not mean they become the leaders of the group. Rather, they represent the group, and only when it is impossible for the whole community or team to gather. In addition, it is sensible to put a fixed period, say 12 months, on their tenure. If at any time an elder does not adequately represent the group, the group – via a normal forum – can remove the elder from his position. Elders are drawn from all ranks. Indeed, rank should have no effect on the decision to elect them. Elders are elected for no reason other than their integrity and wisdom. There must be no lobbying and no candidate discussions. Keep this process simple and be quite sure that people are deciding on their nomination for themselves. One way to achieve this is to give no warning of the election.

Even if people are pre-warned, and if they are aware of the power of the elders, they are very unlikely to elect an inappropriate bully to the position. Carefully explain an elder's function to the people. Let them know that elders have the power to dismiss people. This is a sobering thought, but common sense and the natural goodness of human nature always win through.

It is important to emphasize that the elders will be called only for very serious matters. Routine issues are handled as a matter of course, during the regular monthly *umhlanganos*. However, if the elders are convened, they arrive with only one thing in mind: to protect the community values.

Elders do not all have to come from the affected environment, as they will be protecting the values for which they are accountable and responsible to the community. A group of between seven and nine elders normally works very well, the majority of which must be from the affected team. If this is not the case, there is the risk of infringing one of the most basic interactive leadership rules: the *umhlangano* can only make decision on matters for which it is responsible and accountable.

Elders from other areas in the business may, for example, decide to discipline an individual in a soft manner, whereas the affected group may have been far more severe. As the 'outside' elders are not directly affected (that is, they are not responsible and accountable for the particular work area), they should be used to counsel. The final outcome may be clearly dependent on the affected community representatives.

The inquiry procedure for elders is very simple. They decide everything and are fully accountable to their colleagues. They may make whatever decisions they wish. This premise is based on the traditional African legal system. As HO Moning notes in *The Pedi*, 'usually the verdicts of courts include orders for restitution as well as for punishment, which are decided on simultaneously after a single trial.' The facilitator is only present to ensure the correct procedure is followed. It is important to note that the paradigm used here is the issue under investigation, not the individual.

The elders' inquiry/hearing process

1. Introduction by the person calling the inquiry. (This is normally the manager). The person under scrutiny is present.
2. Run through a list of all complaints.
3. Review each complaint. The person under scrutiny has the opportunity to respond or defend. This is the inquiry stage.
4. Once all the complaints have been discussed, both the person under scrutiny and the manager are asked to leave the room.
5. The elders discuss the connection between the problems discussed and the values infringed. They call any witnesses they may need.
6. The person under scrutiny and the manager return and they are told of any value infringements. Additional questions may be asked by the person, the manager and the elders.
7. The person under scrutiny and the manager leave again.
8. The elders discuss an appropriate course of action.
9. The person under scrutiny and the manager return and are informed of the outcome.

Note: A non-participatory facilitator must be present at all elders' hearings. Each time there is a deadlock of any kind, a secret vote must be taken on the options for the group, to determine the next step. This is always a secret ballot and everyone must vote. A simple majority carries.

It is important to emphasize that the elders must analyse all issues in terms of values. If there is no connection to values, they are not responsible or accountable. However, this will very seldom, if ever, be the case.

To illustrate this, an example of the connections between problem behaviours and value infringements is given below. We must assume that the values listed have been created and are part of an existing group culture.

Problem	Value infringement
Individual talking behind others' backs. Negatively politicking.	Openness, honesty, friendliness
Lack of punctuality	Effectiveness, professionalism
Racial, sexual or other discrimination	Non-discrimination
Poor performance	Effectiveness, professionalism, care, team driven

Whether it is the elders or the entire *umhlangano* that conduct an evaluation, they are fully responsible and accountable for the action they decide to take. They could decide to demote an individual or request a public apology; they can even dismiss an individual. The power rests in their hands along with the joy and responsibility of knowing that they are accountable to themselves and each other. If, for example, the solution fails, the group will have to deal with the failure. If this is not realized, they have somehow ducked their accountability in the process.

In real terms, the community is accountable for upholding the values and, therefore, the culture of the group. However, the ultimate hierarchical leader – the CEO in business, the president of a nation – remains the guardian of the culture. It will be up to him or her to stimulate *umhlanganos*, to discuss particular values when he believes there is a danger of them being eroded or shifted. This will be done through normal command structures, as it is the people who determine what the values mean.

Problem 2: Creeping autocracy

A senior leader can side-step a need to confront his own behaviour and avoid change. By this I mean that there may not be a public *umhlangano* majority of people who have expressed a problem with this senior leader – but there is still a problem which the people discuss privately among themselves. This is particularly relevant to senior management, and a structure and system needs to be put in place to avoid it.

I believe there will be broad agreement that a greater effect will be felt on the organization should an issue be raised by the managing director (MD) rather than the most junior member of staff. Likewise, an infringement of behaviour will be more noticeable and influential if it is executed by the MD rather than the junior. If this is so, the rules governing the behaviour of senior individuals need to be different from, and possibly more strenuous than, those lower down the hierarchy.

For the following discussion, we will need to assume that the value 'non-discriminatory' is accepted by and in place in the community. Let's take, for example, sexist behaviour and language. Pete is sexist. He works in a production team comprising seven people, four of whom are female and the rest male. The issue can be raised and addressed by that group in their own *umhlangano*, but it is likely that when the issue is raised, the majority will support the individual who says that he or she has a problem with Pete's sexism. The issue will be addressed by the *umhlangano* and solved following the normal counselling process (see page 108).

But let's go up a rank to John, the production manager. We need to set the scene for ease of understanding. Please note that I am positioning males in this team fairly negatively as, at least, latent sexists. It is only an example used for illustrative purposes and no insult is intended.

Problems/special situations

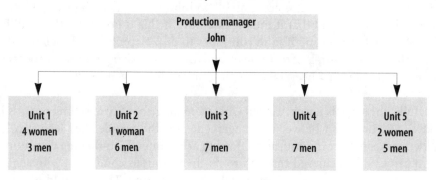

In total, there are seven females in a department of 36 people. In this case, John, the production manager, is also sexist.

Pete's sexism has been addressed by Unit 1 and his behaviour is adjusting accordingly. But all the females – including those in Pete's team – and some of the males, are directly affected and offended by John's sexist behaviour and language. If someone raises this in a general *umhlangano,* it is unlikely – given the composition of the department – that there will be majority support for the concern. This could mean that very little will be done to address the production manager's blatant infringement of the value 'non-discriminatory'. In turn, this will encourage sexism. If John is a leader, people will follow him and may attempt to emulate his behaviour. So what can be done?

The steps taken in this situation are very similar to the normal counselling process for colleagues. However, because senior leadership is involved, the rules are more onerous.

Leadership/management counselling process

▲ The issue is raised as follows: 'I have a problem with John. I don't know if it is an entirely personal problem or if it is one that affects the whole group.' If John is the facilitator, he must to step down immediately and a neutral individual, preferably someone from human resources, should be asked to join the session as facilitator.

▲ The facilitator asks John to leave the room.

▲ The problem is discussed.

▲ A secret vote is held to establish how many people share the concern. If more than five per cent of the people present share the problem, it will have to be raised as a community concern.

▲ The problem behaviour must be connected to a value infringement.

▲ A spokesperson is selected.

▲ John is brought back into the forum, reminded of the values, and the problems are addressed. He is asked to revise his behaviour.

▲ The forum is told that it is accountable to John for his growth through interactive leadership and that it must guide him. If this is not done, they will be answerable to the group if John continues to display problematic behaviour.

▲ End the session with a 'care' value discussion, emphasizing that this process is constructive and has been raised with John's well-being at heart.

Hopefully, the stage is never reached where a management counselling process is needed. Such conflict between management and the people they lead can be avoided by keeping communication flowing at all times. Free-flowing communication can best be achieved through roots-up appraisals conducted with senior management by the various teams to which they belong. These should occur at least once every six months.

Managers belong to several teams. For example, the MD of a company has a senior management group, an office group (which includes everyone at head office), the complete line management structure and, of course, the entire company. It may be difficult to draw certain of these elements together, but this should not be seen as an obstacle. In this case, the MD would have four appraisals every six months. With the permission of the people, this could be adjusted slightly. Perhaps the first three teams could appraise him once every six months and the entire company once a year. It must, nevertheless, be done.

Let's take the sales director as another example. He belongs to the senior management team but does not lead it. Therefore they do not appraise him. He belongs to the sales team which he leads. He also belongs to the office team which includes everyone where he is based. He will have at least two appraisals at least once every six months.

The upside is wonderful as the community responds with constructive input and helps to grow the most senior leaders in the groups. However, they will also raise all the problems and the weaknesses that they perceive. Remember that only five per cent of those present need to share the concern for it to be raised as a community problem. There can be no retribution as the issues were raised openly in the *umhlangano*. The entire group knows that, at any sign of threat or retribution, an emergency management counselling *umhlangano* will be held. At this *umhlangano*, all the elders and as many of the group members as possible will be present. This meeting would be treated as a hearing and the MD, if found guilty, would face severe censure from the community. Dismissal is a possibility.

We need to bear in mind that the rules differ for the leader as we are working on the premise that the more senior one is in the organization or team, the greater the effect of one's actions at the rock-face. In other words, a slight shake of the head in a very senior role will create an enormous ripple at the lower end of the organization.

Roots-up leadership appraisal
▲ Preparation for the appraisal involves ensuring that there is an appropriate facilitator present.
▲ A normal *umhlangano* is formed.
▲ Commence the session by reminding everyone of the shared values by asking them to call out a few. Every now and then, stop on a value and ask people to describe what it means to them. This should take about five minutes. Be sure to end with the value 'Care', to emphasise the positive, constructive nature of the process.
▲ Now remind everyone that it is an appraisal *umhlangano*.
▲ Ask the manager concerned to leave the *umhlangano*.
▲ Remind everyone that if any issue raised as a weakness has at least five per cent support, it will be conveyed to the manager as a community concern. Strengths must have in excess of 51 per cent support.
▲ Begin by asking for the manager's strengths. Write every one called out on the flipchart, without discussion.
▲ Deal with weaknesses in the same way.
▲ Return to the strengths and discuss and vote on each one. Compile a new list of only those that are accepted by the community (that have majority support).
▲ Move to weaknesses and discuss and vote on each one. Compile a list of only those that are accepted by the community (those that have support of more than five per cent).
▲ Call in the manager. The community spokesperson must go through each strength and explain what it means to the community.
▲ Now go through each weakness and explain what they mean to the community.
▲ No examples should be expressed. This avoids the possibility of retribution. The manager must deal with the principle concerned.
▲ Tell the manager that the objective of the appraisal is to grow him, and that everyone in the community cares.

You will notice that we ended on the manager's weaknesses. This is intentional as these are the things on which he should focus. He is also more capable of facing a rather sharp appraisal than a less mature, junior individual. At the same time, he should be building on his strengths. Offer him encouragement.

The community has spoken and the manager must not try to justify or explain away his weaknesses or problems. No litigation is permitted. He must deal with his weaknesses.

Let the manager have a written list of his community-appraised strengths and weaknesses. I keep mine in the front of my diary so that I am constantly reminded of them. Hopefully the person will address them and improve before the next appraisal.

If it were not for this stipulated appraisal, a leader in a senior role, be it the managing director or a manager of a department, can quite easily get away with reprehensible behaviour. Such behaviour could be affecting many people in his community. It is therefore crucial that the community understands the nature and workings of these appraisals in detail . They must understand that the leader is accountable to them and that they can call for an appraisal of the leader if issues appear to have been forgotten.

In conclusion, senior leadership accountability takes into consideration the enhanced position of influence. Essentially, the more senior one is, the more 'perfect' one has to be. Roots-up appraisals emphasize that a shared community concern regarding behaviour is sufficient to activate public guidance and, where necessary, even chastisement.

Criticizing a leader is completely in tune with traditional African culture. Criticism was a pillar of tribal society, but it had to be done in such a way that the leader could not fight back. It was done out of care, and to grow and guide the leader. However, in a traditional society, one did not criticize the leader brutally. It was done gently and poetically – often through praise poetry. King Cetshwayo was reprimanded in this way for seducing a number of other men's wives. It was raised overtly and loudly for all to hear by the praise singer, which made it impossible for him to ignore the issues. Subsequently, he changed his behaviour! Similarly, in Shaka's praise poetry, there is similar behavioural censure. Here is an example:

Zulu	English
Umlilo wotate kaMjokwana.	The fire that burnt *Okamjokwane kandbaba* (Shaka's praise name).
Umlilo wotate ubuhanguhangu.	The fire that ran like an inferno.
Oshise izikova zaseDlebe.	It burnt the owl that was at Dlebe.
Kwaze kwasha nezasemaBedlane.	As well as the ones that were at Mabedlane.

In this praise poem, Shaka is referred to as a fierce bush-fire. It refers to his terrible habit of killing women and other non-combatants in war.

Indeed, if the people did not criticize a leader, he would take issue with the *ibandla* (tribal council). Shaka had several *indunas* (headmen) executed for not opposing decisions which later brought serious consequences to him and the tribe.

Executing staff for lack of criticism may be taking things a little too far! But they need to know that they will have to answer to the community if they do not raise any problems and expose any weaknesses of which they are aware.

PART 5

CHAPTER 13

▲▲▲▲

Interactive leadership unravelled

The thrust of interactive leadership is to develop each individual by demanding accountability, and leadership of himself, his peers and his own leaders. Because of the drive towards community, people can easily become confused about who actually leads an organization or certain dimensions of it. This needs to be clarified.

Values are no particular individual's domain. They are created by the group, and it is the group that becomes accountable for living the values: to ensure they are upheld or to discipline when they are not. The leader is expected to be exemplary, to lead strongly and effectively, but always with the values as a guide.

Purely professional functions are largely the domain of a normal hierarchical leadership structure. After all, it is the leader/manager who conducts individual performance appraisals and decides on financial rewards – not the group. However, there are very few purely professional issues that do not relate to a value and, therefore, to the group.

Because of the environment of trust, openness and respect – all of which are created in the interactive leadership process – the leader will have tremendously enhanced power. He will be able to lead strongly and professionally, and demand extremely high standards without ever encountering resistance from the people. The reason for this is simple to understand. In the process of interactive leadership, one works hard at breaking down barriers between people and between classes. This is physically reflected in *umhlanganos* where each person, regardless of rank, has the same opportunity to contribute their opinion, and to encourage or even stimulate discipline of an individual or the group.

Other realities unfold in the *umhlanganos*. To lead in a strong community, where challenge is encouraged, where there are no holy cows, leaders have to be dynamic and strong. Above all, they have to be good people. Without strong *seriti/isithunzi*, they will not be leaders for long. They will try to revert to autocracy to maintain authority but the people will not allow it. Only the power, the *seriti/isithunzi*, that comes from within a leader will enable that leader to lead.

In the *umhlangano* – like everyone else – the leader is exposed. If, through exposure or lack of it, he does not measure up to the leadership needs of the people, and if he does not retain their respect when vulnerable, he will be unable to lead them professionally. If, however, he retains their respect through that vulnerability, his *seriti/isithunzi* grows and his professional leadership will produce no conflict. The people will trust him and his judgement.

In other words, there are two superimposed structures which are at work constantly, and there is a dynamic tension between them. One is a classic hierarchical leadership structure and the other is a community structure. People belong to both structures simultaneously.

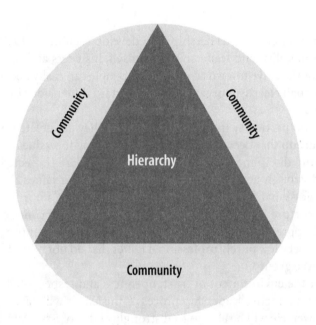

Values are the firm base for both structures. They can be placed on a continuum with corresponding accountability which will be intuitively recognized by all. Although I do not believe one should formalize such a structure, as overstructuring takes away from community sharing, a few examples are given below.

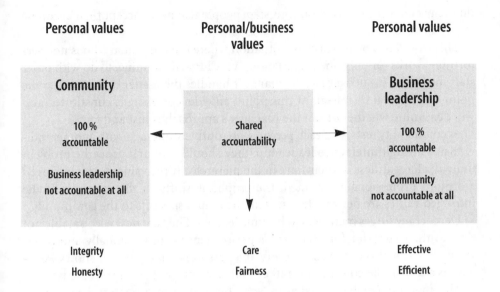

Personal values	Personal/business values	Personal values
Community		**Business leadership**
100 % accountable	Shared accountability	100 % accountable
Business leadership not accountable at all		Community not accountable at all
Integrity	Care	Effective
Honesty	Fairness	Efficient

In this example, integrity and honesty lean towards personal values for which the community is more accountable than business leadership. Likewise, effectiveness and efficiency lean towards business values for which business leadership is more accountable than the community.

As business leadership is part of the community, these leaders will always participate in value assessments and discussions of personal values. Accountability for these belongs to the community. However, values related to business, professionalism and performance will normally form part of business leadership accountability.

I state 'normally' as there will sometimes be interesting anomalies. Let's assume a switchboard operator or receptionist is really inefficient. She is given additional training, but when nothing improves, she is warned by her manager. Even after additional verbal and written warnings, things are not improving. Should he dismiss her? Is he accountable? The classic answer would be: Yes! This is a professional issue and she is not performing at the required standard. However, her role as switchboard operator implies that everyone in the business has something to do with her, and they will all have an informed opinion of the individual's professional capabilities. More importantly, interactive leadership demands that we are accountable to one another for the values we create. Professionalism, in some form, is sure to be one of the values, and everyone shares interactively at all levels in leading the business professionally. The manager may have done everything possible to grow the person, and should call for a community hearing. Everyone is directly affected by the person. Because they can see and hear the problem, and do something about it themselves, the community must decide on the person's future. Without this step, people will never accept their accountability to others.

This would not be the case in a situation where the individual who is not performing works for only one person or has very little, if anything, to do with other staff members. In such a case, the manager handles the matter on his own to the point of potential dismissal. At this point, an elders' hearing is constituted and will determine whether or not the manager's approach is just and fair.

Accountability rests with each person who routinely interacts with another individual. Through interactive leadership, they should lead and grow the problem individual, regardless of their rank in the hierarchy. If the values being infringed are more professionally oriented, the emphasis shifts to the manager. If the infringed values are personally oriented, the emphasis shifts to the community.

Democracy forces managers to become leaders. They are now accountable not only to their superior for their staff's performance – professionally and behaviourally – but also to the community. If a person is unassertive or shows weakness as a leader, the community, rather than a superior, may address the issue.

This method may be viewed as unworkable and clumsy, but, on the contrary, it makes for tremendous efficiency and effectiveness. The hierarchical leader remains accountable for leading his people, but the method of leadership is now interactive. He has to be an excellent leader, a good person and a real professional at his job function.

If we do not endorse democracy in business, why do we insist on it for our nation? Is it because, in the nation, we are just simple citizens who fear and decry autocracy? We demand accountability from our political and government leaders. We demand openness. However, in business we have the opportunity to dictate, to be the autocratic ruler ourselves. On this basis, autocracy appears easier to accept. In other words, if we are in power, autocracy works; but if we are not in power, democracy is critical! Is this a fair reflection? Perhaps all we really want is strong, accountable leadership that we can trust without fear.

For example, the British SAS are considered a highly disciplined, efficient and effective group. Not surprisingly, they share this interactive philosophy in selecting leaders.

Officers joining the SAS do so only after they have faced a barrage of withering criticism from other ranks, and restructured their own thinking about the men with whom they will soldier.

A further result has been to foster a unique military democracy within the SAS in which, if he succeeds, a man exchanges his former class and even identity for membership of a caste as binding as any family, and expulsion from which, therefore, becomes the only sanction he really fears.

– J GERAGHTY, *Who Dares Wins*

Strong leadership is important within a democracy. The manager is still account-able. He is still expected to act strongly and professionally, but he must know that he needs to do things for the right reasons. He is forced to be real, to be open and honest, to show respect for knowledgeable people around him, to be an excellent leader.

Sceptics will argue that the real world is not like the SAS, that it is not one great big specialist unit, and that we need the normal 'army' in business. My belief is that every person is capable of unbelievable achievements and that the under-development of individuals – of human resources – is a direct reflection on inad-equate leadership.

Special forces still need clerks and dishwashers, but they are all accountable to themselves and each other, and are proud to be where they are. They are all de-veloped as the very best clerks and dishwashers in the world.

African interactive leadership is not dependent on blackness or whiteness. It is based on humanity. It is expressed in the Now African who draws on a collective heritage of powerful community (*ubuntu*), a sophisticated sense of self (*seri-ti/isithunzi*) and the warrior ethics of rugged determination, complete prepared-ness, discipline, loyalty and respect. These features rest as comfortably with a white African as they do with a black African. There is no need to debate whether these features still exist in the African people of today. Accept to a greater or lesser degree it still does – in some places very strongly, while in others only as an echo of the past. The issue is rather what to do about it.

As we explored earlier, using Japan and Hitler's Germany as examples, a busi-ness or a nation can decide on the nature of its culture. Values can be actively and aggressively marketed. But which values? To avoid outrage and perversion, they need to be democratically decided on by the people. Values will only remain intact if accountability for them remains with the people. For people to achieve and to become fully empowered, we must nurture and develop African interactive leadership. It takes us beyond simple accountability for tasks into the realm of accountability for mutual development.

South African business, and the nation as a whole, is in the unique position of now being able to decide what our culture should be. As businesses are a micro-cosm of our nation, they should be synergized with the national vision. We are in the New South Africa: the 'rainbow nation' of cultures, religions and philosophies. It is a new democracy that pursues consensus, inclusivity and transparency in all it does. But it is one that exists outside of business. The African way – African Inter-active Leadership – can become the means to develop, through business, a nation and a continent of winners.

It is our attitude to leadership that will dictate achievement or the lack of it. Interactively, through the community, *ubuntu, seriti/isithunzi* and the warrior leader inside every one of us, anything is possible!

References

Becker, P: *Hill of Destiny,* Penguin, 1969.

Becker, P: *Path of Blood,* Penguin, 1962.

Berglund, A-I: *Zulu Thought Patterns and Symbolism,* David Philip, 1989.

Bonner, P: Kings, *Commoners and Concessionaires,* Ravan Press, 1983.

Brandt, SC: *Strategic Planning in Emerging Companies,* Addison-Wesley, 1981.

Clothier, N: *Black Valour,* University of Natal Press, 1987.

Cole, B: *The Elite – The Rhodesian Special Air Service,* Three Knights Publishing, 1984.

Covey, SR: *The Seven Habits of Highly Effective People,* Simon & Shuster, 1989.

Crosby, PB: *The Eternally Successful Organisation,* New American Library, 1988.

Delius, P: *The Land Belongs to Us,* Ravan Press, 1983.

Geraghty, T: *Who Dares Wins,* Fontana Collins, 1980.

Hammond-Tooke, D: *The Roots of Black South Africa,* Jonathan Ball, 1993.

Hancock, G: *Lords of Poverty,* Macmillan, 1989.

Jordaan, J: *Population Growth – Our Time Bomb,* JL van Schaik, 1991.

Krige, EJ: *The Social System of the Zulus,* Shuter & Shooter, 1950.

Kunene, M: *Emperor Shaka the Great,* Heinemann, 1979.

Langer, WL (ed): *Western Civilisation – The Expansion to Europe in the Modern World,* Harper & Row, 1968.

Ley, WF and C Murray: *Transformations on the Highveld: The Tswana and Southern Sotho,* David Philip, 1980.

Monnig, HO: *The Pedi,* JL van Schaik, 1967.

Mostert, N: *Frontiers,* Jonathan Cape, 1992.

Muller, CFJ (ed): *500 Years – A History of South Africa,* Human and Rousseau Academica, 1981.

Musashi, M: *The Book of Five Rings,* Bantam Books, 1982.

Myburgh, AC (ed): *Anthropology for Southern Africa,* JL van Schaik, 1981.

Nitobe, I: *Bushido – The Soul of Japan,* Charles E Tuttle Company Inc, 1969.

Nyembezi, CLS: *Zulu Proverbs,* Shuter & Shooter, 1990.

Pascale, RT and AG Athos: *The Art of Japanese Management,* Penguin, 1981.

Peck, MS: *The Different Drum,* Arrow Books, 1987.

Radice, B: *Aristotle: The Politics,* Penguin, 1962.

Ritter, EA: *Shaka Zulu,* Penguin, 1955.

Robbins, SP: *Essentials of Organizational Behaviour,* Prentice Hall, 1984.

Saayman, G: *Modern South Africa in Search of Soul,* Sisa Sternback, 1990.

Schapera, I: *The Tswana,* KPI Limited, 1984.

Schram, S: *Mao Tse-Tung,* Penguin, 1966.

Schutte, A: *Philosophy for Africa,* University of Cape Town Press, Cape Town, 1993.

Shillington, K: *The Colonisation of the Southern Tswana 1870–1900,* Ravan Press, 1985.

Spiegel, AD and PA McAllister (eds): *Tradition and Transition in Southern Africa,* Witwatersrand University Press, 1991.

Stapleton, TJ: *Maqoma Xhosa Resistance to Colonial Advance,* Jonathan Ball, 1994.

Stuart, J and D McK Malcolm (eds): *The Diary of Henry Francis Fynn,* Shuter & Shooter, 1986.

Tempels, P: *Bantu Philosophy,* Présence Africaine, 1959.

Theal, GM: *History of South Africa Since 1795,* C Struik, 1964.

Thompson, L (ed): *African Societies in Southern Africa,* Heinemann, 1969.

Twala, M and E Benard: *Mbokodo Inside MK,* Jonathan Ball, 1994.

Wilson, M and L Thompson: *A History of South Africa to 1870,* David Philip, 1982.

Young, P (ed): *Strategy and Tactics of the Great Generals and Their Battles,* Bison Books, 1984.

The World's Religions, Lion Publishing, 1982.

About the author

Chunge Chunge
He who achieves even though the road be difficult and torturous
iNdlandlo eyafihla iKhanda eGoli
The mamba that hid its head in Johannesburg
Yavela ngomsila eKaba
And its tail can be seen in the Cape
Ukhozi iwentaba kalukhuzeki
The raptor of the mountain which cannot be tamed
Nhliziyo dela wena osufikile phezulu
Whose heart is only content when he has reached the top

— Zulu praises

Mike Boon is the Executive Chairman of Group Africa of the Amavulandlela which operates companies in rural and urban areas. He is a member of the Young Presidents' Organization. He was born in a rural area in KwaZulu-Natal, where, during his growing years, he developed a deep love and understanding of all the peoples of South Africa. His business experience has taken him into deep rural and traditional areas as well as into the heart of the townships. He has a passion for the music and dance of township and traditional people.

As a leader, Mike feels strongly that leadership is a responsibility to help all those with whom one comes into contact. He feels passionate about his business and through it hopes to encourage people to respect differences and to live together in harmony.

About Group Africa

Group Africa of the Amavulandlela (the pathfinders) is a happy, productive, exciting, interesting and profitable African business which has discarded the rule books and, in so doing, has discovered a truly powerful African way. Its primary business is as an integrated communications agency and media operator. This agency communicates with 3,5-million people, face-to-face, every month in South Africa alone. It also has companies in the travel industry, and in film and television commercial productions.

It is a small-to-medium sized, but highly successful, enterprise that culturally, racially and religiously is a very close profile of the entire community: there are urban and rural people, wealthy and poor, well-educated and illiterate. There are First World and tribal people and there are even Third World chancers! Yet they are a wonderful team with a 'family' structure that shares a very special culture. That culture was formed during the height of the apartheid years. It weathered township and rural violence, and tribal faction fighting in the name of politics. It contributed to the formation of the new South Africa by educating millions of people about democracy and peace. There is trust, respect and pride in who and what they are, and in what they do.

Group Africa of the Amavulandlela has reflected a compounded growth of 60 per cent each year for 10 consecutive years, and has directly assisted in growing and improving the life of everyone who works there. Group Africa is a particularly unusual company which is governed interactively and with mutual respect.

Group Africa believes that the workplace should reflect personal values and be in harmony with belief systems – after all, we spend around 80 per cent of our waking lives at work. The workplace should be the vehicle through and in which everyone is able to achieve their personal aspirations.

At the risk of appearing less than humble, this is what some clients have said about Group Africa:

What impressed me most was the commitment and sincerity of the staff of Group Africa. You all seem to combine an almost evangelical fervour to explain the richness of African culture with some sound business pragmatism! Quite unique in my experience.

– GAVIN NEATH, MANAGING DIRECTOR, LEVER PONDS

I was very impressed by the authenticity of the character of the presentation. You did not confirm my suspicion that whenever white people talk about Africans, they look on racial stereotypes. You also displayed the inner feeling on the spirit of being African in South Africa in this century. At no stage did I feel uncomfortable with the cultural aspect of the materials presented.
　– BHABHALAZI BULUNGU, PERSONNEL MANAGER, GILETTE SOUTH AFRICA

Well done, your efforts are an inspiration to the marketing industry'
　　　– JOHN MONTGOMERY, DIRECTOR, OGILVY & MATHER

Index

A
Abasekunene 28
abuntu people: philosophy of 31–4
accountability 65, 75, 81, 82, 83, 90, 95,
    96, 100, 102, 106–14, 118, 120, 122,
    124, 127, 128, 129, 130, 131; to self
    97–105
amaBhele 28
amabhinca 47
amagxaxga 47
amaHlubi 27, 28
amakholwa 47, 48
amaNgwane 25, 27
amaZizi 28
ancestors, *see* shades
ancestry 17, 18, 19, 23, 25, 35
appraisal: mutual 112–13; leadership
    123–4
autocracy 68–9, 72, 73, 74, 75, 82, 85, 92,
    108, 120, 130

B
Bafokeng 28
Batlokwa 28
behaviour 63–6
Bhaca 28
Boers 29, 30

C
captains 99, 100, 101, 102, 103
coaches 99, 101, 103
communication 122; use and misuse of
    63–6
community 34, 35, 44, 45, 46, 48, 67–76,
    89, 93, 95, 100, 117, 118, 120, 121, 123,
    124, 127, 128, 129, 130
conflict 31, 47–53, 58, 59, 60–3, 67, 68, 73,
    74, 91, 93, 122

consensus 74–6, 83, 90, 95
counselling process: for employees
    109–10; for management 121–2
customs 15
culture 15, 16, 20, 21, 22, 25, 31, 37, 43, 44,
    47, 48, 52, 53, 57, 65, 86, 87, 91, 106,
    119, 120, 131

D
democracy 74, 82, 83, 85, 88–96, 103, 108,
    113
Difaqane 25, 29
Dingiswayo 25, 26
discipline 19, 42, 43, 44, 48, 50, 52, 66, 72,
    76, 111, 118, 127, 130, 131
discussion groups, *see umhlangano*

E
elders 117–18, 122; inquiry/hearing
    process 119–20
Erasmus, Stephanus 29
ethics 33, 50
ethnicity 60–3
Ethnicity/needs model 61

F
facilitators 118, 119, 121
family 34, 36, 84, 89
First World values 49, 50, 52

G
goals 106
Great Trek 29
group 32, 34, 36, 42, 57, 69, 86, 95, 99,
    100, 102, 107, 108, 111, 117, 118, 120,
    121, 122, 127, 130
Griqua 26
Group Africa 17, 22, 23, 36, 37, 44, 89, 90

H
Hancock, Graham 49, 50
Hintsa 28
history 15, 17, 19, 25–30, 36, 52, 87, 91

I
idlozi, see shades
impimpi 99
individual, the 35, 36, 38, 39, 44, 60, 83, 100, 102, 106, 107, 127, 131
industrial relations 58–9
intellectualism 63–4; use and misuse of 63–6
interactive forums, *see umhlangano*
interactive leadership 80–3, 95, 96, 97, 104, 112, 122, 127–31
isiduko 18
isithunzi, see *seriti/isithunzi*
izibongos 18

J
Japanese management systems 15, 16, 37, 38, 43, 44, 74, 131
justice 67–76

K
kidiboko 18
Kruger, Paul 30

L
law 67–76
leadership 15, 16, 25, 39, 43, 50, 51, 57, 60, 65, 68–9, 69–70, 71, 72, 86, 89, 91, 93, 94, 95, 100, 101, 102–5, 110, 111, 112, 113, 120, 124, 127, 128, 129, 131; counselling process 121–2; model of 98, 102; progression of 98–101; roots-up appraisal 123–4; tribal 44–6
loyalty 73, 89, 93, 131

M
Madikane 28

Makwana 27
Malaysia 15, 16, 74
management 39, 58, 59, 60, 71, 81, 85, 89, 90, 91, 93, 96, 99, 103, 104, 107, 108–12, 113, 119, 120, 121, 123, 124, 127, 130; counselling process 121–2
Mandela, Nelson 16, 36, 66, 68, 72
Manthatisi 27, 28
Maqoma 25
Maslow's hierachy of needs 61
Matiwane 27, 29
Mfecane 25, 30
Mfengu 28
Mkalipi 30
mob rule 74–6
Moshoeshoe 28, 29
Mpangazitha 27, 28
Mthetwa 25
mutual appraisal 112–13
Mutwa, Credo 19, 20, 35, 43
Mzilikazi 27, 29, 30

N
narrowing the grey 93–6
Ndelbele 27, 29, 30
Ndwandwe 25, 26
Ngqika 25
Nguni 26
Nkagarahanye 27
nyangas 21–4

O
oral traditions 65

P
participation 68–71
players 99, 100
Potgieter, Hendrik 29
principles 84–5
problems: dealing with 117–24
productivity 15, 43, 58, 59, 60, 67, 68, 84, 108

R

representation 117–20

S

Sandile 25
sangomas 19, 21
Sebetwane 27
self 35–46
seriti/isithunzi 35–7, 38, 44, 70, 74, 81,
    100, 106, 113, 127, 128, 131
shades 19–21, 22, 23, 24, 35
shadow 42, 44
Shaka 18, 25, 26, 27, 29, 76, 124
Shangaan 27
sharing 88–96
Singapore 15, 74
Sobhuza 26
Soshangane 27
Sotho 26
spectators 99, 100

T

Takers 48, 49, 50, 51, 53, 63, 65
team 44, 85, 105, 113, 118, 119;
    importance of 71–4
Tembu 28
Third World Takers, *see* Takers
time: concepts of 17–19
training 60
tribal leadership 44–6
tribe 30, 47–53, 60–3, 73, 84
Tshane 27
Tswana 26

U

ubuntu 31–4, 44, 68, 74, 90, 95, 104, 108,
    131; manifestations of 33–4, 48
umbango 91, 107
umhlangano 89–91, 92, 95, 96, 97, 102,
    104, 107, 108–12, 113, 118, 120, 121,
    122, 123, 127
uMona 99, 107

V

values 16, 33, 43, 49, 68, 72, 75, 84–5, 89,
    90, 92, 93, 94, 95, 96, 97, 102, 108, 110,
    113, 117, 122, 123, 127, 128, 129, 130;
    creation of 85–7, 91–3; First World
    49, 50, 52; infringement of 119, 121
vision 74, 79
Voortrekkers 29, 30
vulnerability 72, 82, 97, 100, 128
Vusani 28

W

warrior, ethic of 37–44
what we are 57–66
what we can become 79–87
work ethic 60
work groups 59–60
workers 58, 59

X

Xhosa 25, 28

Z

Zulu 25, 26
Zwangendaba 27
Zwide 25